The
New Scriabin
ENIGMA AND ANSWERS

The
New Scriabin
ENIGMA AND ANSWERS
Faubion Bowers

St. Martin's Press   New York

To
ALAN MARKS
and
RUTH RENDLEMAN

Contents

Charcoal sketch of Scriabin by N. P. Ulyanov, begun in 1914 and completed in 1916

Introduction

VLADIMIR ASHKENAZY

I consider Scriabin one of the greatest composers. Of course, it is not easy to support such a statement about anyone. But it is my opinion. He had a unique idiom which is full of meaning, at least to me, and I, for one, am convinced of Scriabin's greatness. It has been a long time now for Scriabin to come into his own in the West.

In Russia Scriabin is better known and better understood. There he is a national heritage. Sooner or later one is faced with his music, and this usually occurs in one's teens. One friend of mine, the man who got me interested first in Scriabin, was so dedicated a Scriabinist that he visited the Scriabin Museum ten times a week. I went through this stage of Scriabin mania, too. In the end, as it should, the passion subsided. But the knowledge and affection remain to this day.

Scriabin's philosophical ideas do not, however, make a desirable impact on me. Scriabin himself shows considerable confusion here. I think his idea of a universal transformation of the world through art naive. But one must still remember that the basis of his thought was indestructible faith and loyalty to Art as a means of elevating man's spirit and of showing light, goodness, and truth. He may not have transformed the world, but he made one person better at least. Myself.

No one knows whether Scriabin's music would have been the same had he not been possessed by his visions. I suspect it would not. Although one cannot say that without understanding his philosophy one cannot understand the music, one penetrates deeper into his music, if one studies what compelled Scriabin. One cannot separate the man-as-philosopher from the composer of such beautiful music. His music has a unique idealism. It has its own laws and its own meaning. His workmanship was nearly always impeccable. He continues to be a fascinating and controversial figure in musical history, and a man about whom opinions will always differ.

Preface

Virtually all of the material in this short, critical biography
of the Russian composer Alexander Nikolaevich Scriabin
(1871–1915) is new to readers outside the Soviet Union.
Some of it is new even to those in Russia. I at last have
used materials supplied to me in private correspondence
with various musicologists and Scriabinists but withheld
from my earlier, two-volume book, *Scriabin*. Further, because of the centenary celebrations in Russia throughout
the year 1972, and in consequence of ever-widening hon-
esty about musical matters there, a spate of fresh informa-
tion and anecdote has been released by the Soviets. The
skeleton of Scriabin's life remains immutable, since the
composer is no longer living or writing, but I have fleshed
out details and made correctives and clarifications on the
basis of sources not used in my earlier biography.

My first book on Scriabin was more "materials" than
biography—what Martin Cooper called "a mine of infor-
mation"—in that it consisted of exhaustive, and perhaps
exhausting, translations of letters, documents, poems, texts
and reminiscences. The result was a statue rather than a

life, and I avoided "critical analysis," since this was the
first book in English based on what Scriabin himself actually said, and what his friends and enemies actually said
about him.

Scriabin then was not yet in fashion as he is now, and
I thought he was not ready for a more opinionated or
retrospective evaluator at that time. Naturally, I corrected
in the second and subsequent editions many factual errors
and slips in that work. However, in response to the somewhat surprising and sudden popularity—vogue, even—of
Scriabin's music today, a number of people whose opinions
I trust suggested I take a more incisive look at Scriabin
and write a more basic, generalized book suitable for a
wider readership.

Scriabin's music, like his life itself, poses many questions
and provides few answers. What, for instance, does a
biographer do when confronted with conflicting instances
of trivialities such as these:

He is told that Scriabin habitually spent hours at his
toilette and that he obsessively carried a pocket comb with
him at all times. He would spend an hour brushing, comb-
ing and grooming his hair and mustaches only to preen
again "like a young girl in love" before entering the drawing room where the guests were assembled. Once he nearly
missed a train because he had left a ten-kopeck comb in
his hotel room. And yet on the jacket of this book you see
a formal studio portrait, taken in Leipsig in 1908 by the
Welte-Mignon Company for advertising purposes, showing Scriabin mussed carelessly.

The biographer is informed from several different sources
that Scriabin was terrified of sitting on the grass for fear
of chigger bites. But we have two photographs which show
him seated outdoors—one in youth before his neuroses

seized him so firmly, and one in later life. How much persuasion preceded those bucolic snapshots? One wonders.

And what of more serious matters? What does the biographer do when he explores the possibility of homosexuality as an explanation of Scriabin's person? Robert Craft
in the *New York Times* "concurred . . . as, on page after
page, Scriabin reveals himself to be emotionally hermaphrodite." Yet, Henry-Louis de la Grange in *Music and
Musicians* found only "an inverted impotence complex."

Fortunately, the biographer's task is easy when Scriabin
himself repeatedly says (like Rameau), "There is no difference between harmony and melody. They are one and
the same." Sergei Pavchinsky, an authority who incidentally does not come off well in the succeeding pages,
writes: "Both with the Romantics and with Scriabin of
the Prometheus period, the melody somehow breaks away
from the harmony and takes on the character of an independent scale or tonality . . . Scriabin's melodies are incomparably autonomous and have an entire arsenal of
expressive possibilities on their own." The biographer simply
disputes him. Happily, he can now bring into battle the
howitzers of Varvara Dernova's discoveries which break
the code of Scriabin's harmonic and melodic system. (See
Chapter VIII.)

Any one person is, in short, many people. Each, like refracted light which alters as the source itself alters, changes
at his own pace in his own time and place. Scriabin of
1888 was not Scriabin of 1911. Neither is the biographer
in 1969 the same man in 1973.

Scriabin, perhaps more than any other composer in the
history of music, inspired during his lifetime and continues
to rouse sharp contrasts of opinion—violent hatred or passionate veneration. Opinions about Scriabin are affected by

Scriabin himself traveling perilously between the frontiers of reality and imagination, confusing and causing to be confused fact and fancy. Because his music was so imperative, people tried to believe in Scriabin the man. Those who did often did so at the expense of their own reality . . . and other people's truth.

My very special thanks for help, advice, suggestions, comment and corrections of this present book go to Ellon Carpenter in Ohio, Roy Guenther in Maryland, Vladimir Ashkenazy in Iceland, Bulat Galeev in Kazan, Tatyana Shaborkina in Moscow, and in New York Ruth Rendleman, Gary Keeper and Len Finger who typed the manuscript, and John Ruggero who copied out the musical examples. I am particularly indebted to my editor, Leslie Pockell, for sure-handed guidance.

Hopefully, this book will be an accessible view, an unravelling, of the most mysterious and complex musical personality of this century, one who belongs to every country at any time.

1 Broad Stream: Different Currents

Every artist in history can be comprehended in more than one way, even in several ways at once. Just as no single person possesses the whole of any truth, so too, no one school of individuals nor one country owns the exclusive interpretation of a work of art or its creator, regardless of how sanctifying the shedding graces of tradition, orthodoxy, background, and geographical or historical identity may be.

The Western view of Scriabin differs dramatically and pronouncedly from the Soviet view. The double variant in ways of looking at him—and accepting or rejecting him—as man and as musician unearths a nest of contradictions, many of them seemingly unresolvable. This divergence is reflected in musicological opinions and attitudes, and even in actual performance of the works themselves.

It is natural to an extent for Russia and America or Europe—separated by so many miles in distance and ideology—to take contrasting stands on any event or circumstance. But the matter of Scriabin is more intricately skeined than usual cultural or political differences. If Scriabin's art and thought transcend space and time, why then

1

are responses to it not more unified, if not unanimous?
There really is no argument over Beethoven, say, prefer-
ences aside.

How, for instance, to reconcile the Soviet view that Scriabin's music foreshadowed the Revolution, with the western picture of the theosophical, effete and mad Scriabin
whose music was filled with pointless mysticism? "A messianic miniaturist," Martin Cooper calls him. "Sick and
neurasthenic musician-thaumaturge," émigré Leonid Sabaneeff wrote from France. A composer akin to *"radeniya,*
whose services develop into the orgies of dervish dances,"
Lazare Saminsky called him in America, referring to the
zealousness of Russian religious sects. "Driver of music to
the verge of histrionics," is how Peter Dickinson described
Scriabin. At the height of the Stalinist period in Russia,
Dmitri Shostakovich call Scriabin "an unhealthy and negative phenomenon," while Boris Shteinpress created a new
set of epithets: "Scriabin is a degenerate formalist of the
worst sort . . . listeners should be spared the degrading
experience of having to listen to him."

This man is today widely and wildly popular in Communist Russia, a country where rank by birth has been abolished and where the tenets of Socialist Realism demand
that all art which does not contribute to "the improvement
of mankind" must be discarded. For all his metaphysics,
he still had calling cards printed abroad which read "Alexandre de Scriabine," as if he was more than tenuously
entitled to a title. Still he moved in Russia from being a
symbol of decadence to becoming "a symbol of progres-
siveness" . . . a cosmonautic mascot.

There is really no need to point out Scriabin's promi-
nence in the pantheon of Russian musicians. But first a
word about the development of Russian music. It began
as late as 1836 when Mikhail Glinka's first nationalistic

native, indigenously Russian opera was performed—A *Life
for the Tsar*, so named in order to pass censorship with the
Tsar. Originally, he called it *Ivan Susanin*, as the Soviets
call it again today. Ten years earlier, Glinka had been
writing like a complete foreigner, an Italian or French
musician. He was as he himself said, "a jay bedecked with
other birds' plumage." The 1830's was a time for "fathers"
—the father of Russian drama, Nikolai Gogol; the father
of Russian poetry, Alexander Pushkin; and of course, Mikhail Glinka, the father of Russian music.

Russian music came into its own in the 1860's, just as
there was a burst of genius in literature with Tolstoi, Do-
stoevsky and Turgenev. They were suns within the Russian
universe. So too were the great musicians—Rimsky-Korsakov,
Tchaikovsky, Borodin, Mussorgsky. The world of Russian
music by the 1880's had become spectacular. There was
Tchaikovsky's opera *Eugene Onegin*, his ballet *The Sleep-
ing Beauty*, and his Fifth Symphony. Also, at this time
Rimsky-Korsakov had written his orchestral pieces, "Spanish Caprice" and "Scherezade."

But these nationalist Russian composers were not the
end of Russian musical flowering. The period served merely
as a turning point. Soon came Scriabin and his classmate
Rachmaninov to continue the past. To sharpen the perspective, it might be noted that Scriabin was twenty-one
years of age when Tchaikovsky died and fourteen at the
time of Liszt's death. His first serious compositions were
published in 1897, the year that Brahms died.

Already by 1912, the *Petersburgsky Listok*, a critical journal of music, proclaimed that the first stage of Russian
music was Glinka and (Anton) Rubinstein, the second,
Tchaikovsky, the third, Glazunov and Arensky, and the
fourth, Scriabin. Sergei Prokofiev, a composer whose life
overlapped Scriabin's as Scriabin's overlapped Rimsky's,

somewhat later defined his predecessor as a "broad stream," and swam in Scriabin's waters for a while, as we will see. But perhaps it is in casual asides and unstated assumptions that Scriabin's eminence becomes clearest. Take Nikolai Miaskovsky, for example, a master symphonist whose music is as neglected in the West as it is honored in the USSR. He once made this remark—revelatory of Scriabin—in speaking of himself: "I place Mussorgsky on an equal footing with Tchaikovsky and Scriabin, and reject Glazunov and his whole school, although I myself, unfortunately, am still enmeshed in its nets."

Today's Russians, quite simply, regard Scriabin as a vital current in the mainstream—Prokofiev's "broad stream." Soviet pianist Sviatoslav Richter, for instance, recalls his most formidable and earliest musical experience as that of hearing Heinrich Neuhaus (the "Father of Soviet Pianism" as the cliché goes) play Scriabin's Tenth Sonata Op. 70 in concert. And Russian pyrotechnician Vladimir Ashkenazy, now a citizen of Iceland, remembers—and recaptures in his all-Scriabin recitals—the time when he lived, ate, slept, and breathed "nothing but Scriabin."

The festivities celebrating the one-hundredth anniversary of Scriabin's birth commenced on 6 January, 1972. They were launched officially by the Ministry of Culture and the Union of Soviet Composers with a grand concert at the Great Hall of the Moscow Conservatory. People's Artist and Lenin Prize Winner Dmitri Shostakovich was scheduled to make the opening remarks (ironically enough, after his attacks on Scriabin during Stalinist times). However, for unexplained reasons, his address was read by Rodion Shchedrin, Secretary of the Union of Soviet Composers. Shostakovich described Scriabin as "living and continuing to live for many generations . . . dear to us for his belief in the transforming power of art, for his ability to enrich the soul of man, for bringing harmony into the lives of the people."

Ivan Martynov, one of the two Soviet Members of the International Musicological Congress, lectured on "Scriabin's Creative Work." People's Artist Yevgeni Svetlanov conducted the Moscow Philharmonic in the *Poem of Ecstasy* and Meritorious Artist Stanislav Neuhaus played the Concerto. The concert was by invitation only, and everybody in the musical world except Shostakovich attended. Margarita Fyodorova, leading Scriabinist, played a cycle of Scriabin's complete piano works in six recitals at the Moscow Conservatory soon after.

The Soviets, as part of the year-long celebrations, issued a large, four-kopeck stamp picturing Scriabin in front of a grand piano. They updated and much improved an old record taken from Scriabin's own performances for the Welte-Mignon and Phonola companies made in 1908 and 1912. They issued a batch of records, lettered in gold, with classic performances by Heinrich Neuhaus, his son Stanislav (who does not play nearly so well), and Scriabin's son-in-law, the late Vladimir Sofronitsky, perhaps the best Scriabin performer of recent times.

Sovetskaya Kultura, the official organ of the Ministry of Culture and the Central Committee of the Professional Union of Cultural Workers, gave a front page article to Scriabin titled in heavy print, "PRIDE OF RUSSIAN MUSIC." *Sovetskaya Rossiya*, a daily newspaper in Moscow began a lead article, "Alexander Nikolaevich Scriabin is one of those names Russian art is proud of . . ." The headline blazed out at the reader like a banner: "I have come to tell the people that they are powerful and mighty."

Another journal for the general Soviet citizen, *Ogonyok*,

in its second issue of 1972 contained an article written by M. Kvartsev, who speaks in tones generally reserved for Lenin: "Scriabin loved life as only man can love it, loved it to exaltation, and tenderly and lyrically sang of nature, its colors and moods. He loved people . . . passionately believed in the triumph of light over darkness." Kvartsev is not altogether misreading, or misleading his public. A younger Scriabin did, indeed, speak about these positive things so appropriate to Communist propaganda.

As for the "spread of love for Scriabin ever wider," and his "entering our lives more and more," Tatyana Shaborkina, Director of the Scriabin Museum, explains, "Geniuses are always children of the one family of Mankind. They bring light, joy and life with their creativity. I very much like Scriabin's words, and he felt every life was worthy of becoming the Man Creator, and that man's essence appeared in creativity: 'Life is eternally creative, full of miracles and revelations, ever new and ever deeper, infinite and inexhaustible.'"

Lenin long ago set the tone for drawing positives instead of negatives from the past. "If we have before us," he said, "a truly great artist, then he must represent in his works certain essential aspects of the Revolution even in cases where he does not clearly understand it and openly avoids it." He wrote on another occasion, "Indeed, we Revolutionaries are far from denying the Revolutionary role of the reactionary period [1907–1912, a period of severe repression following the abortive 1905 Revolution]. We understand that types of social movements change, that ideas and thought change, even when political workers themselves are in prison." Lenin's statements are by no means mere casuistry.

To bear him out, take the *Poem of Ecstasy*, for instance, a composition which like most of Scriabin's music, can be described as Harold C. Schonberg of the *New York Times* recently wrote, as "sensuous and even erotic, as much as music can be erotic." Eroticism, of course, is anathema to Socialist Realism and its advocates. Now to Albert Coates, the English conductor at the Imperial Court Opera in Petrograd, quoted in *Musical America* in an interview on May 1, 1919, having "made good his escape from the Bolsheviki":

It is, of course, not the educated public of former days, which has almost entirely disappeared, but a new and entirely democratic public consisting of work-people, peasants, soldiers and sailors. Whatever the "People" do in the political and social sphere, and their record is pretty bad, at concerts they sit reverently . . . They show a marked preference for modern and complicated music, infinitely preferring it to the older and simpler forms of Russian music. Their special favorite, strange as it may seem, is Scriabin, and after a performance of this composer's *Poème d'Extase* that I was conducting, the public, which consisted almost entirely of the "People," shouted themselves hoarse with enthusiasm. This so astonished me (I had never dreamed that they would understand it) that I turned to a sailor who was yelling fit to burst his lungs and asked him what it was he liked so much about the work. "Ah," he said, "I'm of course not wise enough to understand it, but it makes me feel like a young horse. I should love to kick out, and then run around a field for an hour." After this performance I was continually receiving requests—work-people used to stop me in the streets —to get up another concert and conduct *Poème d'Extase*, they wanted so much to hear it.

Victor Delson, in the most recent biography of Scriabin (1971) states clearly the Russian case: "Scriabin's creative work could only have grown out of that soil which nur-

8   *The New Scriabin*

tured the two greatest revolutionary movements of 1905
and 1917 . . . Doubtless, the winds of the symbolist-
decadents touched Scriabin, but they did not determine
the ideas of his creative work, his direction, and historical
significance. Thus, in spite of the theme of doom, the picture of universal death and darkness which developed so
intensively in the art of many symbolist-decadents [during
his lifetime], the music of Scriabin in its whole extent gives
priority to the idea of overcoming obstacles through struggle, presents an insurgent hero striving for happiness and
the victory of light and freedom." He sums up:

> Hence our acceptance today of Scriabin's 'yesteryear' art.
> This most brilliant Russian composer imbibed and expressed
> with extraordinary power and sincerity the emotional red-
> heat of unrest and the protest feelings of people in the
> shadow of intensifying social events. To a notable degree this
> is why his name, the name of this daring innovator, is in-
> scribed in the culture of the present.

And Delson cites as a suitable epigraph for all Scriabin's
oeuvre four lines from a revolutionary poem by Alexander
Blok.

> Oh Spring without end and limitless
> Without end and limitless dream!
> I know you, life! I accept!
> And greet you with the ring of battleshield!

To further his point he also offers us lines from Valeri
Briussov, another symbolist poet but close friend of Scriabin
in his last years. Briussov, like Blok, lived well into the
Revolution and after and also later abandoned prophecies
and clouds of doom:

> The poet is always with the people
> When the thunderstorm sings
> And song and storm are
> Eternal sisters

The association of Scriabin with immediate events existed in the composer's own lifetime long before the Revolution itself. Pianist Anatol Drozdov reminisced for *Soviet Music* magazine in 1946, saying that to Scriabin's contemporaries his music was "a triumphant synthesis of the meaning of art and revolution." The esteemed critic Boris Asafiev reflected in his 1968 history of Russian music: "The music of Scriabin is the unrestrained, deeply human striving toward freedom and happiness, the struggle toward life's delights." And Vladimir Sofronitsky once described Scriabin this way: "Life, light, struggle—that is where Scriabin's true greatness lies," placing him well within those Party-line "progressive, humanistic, living ideals" promulgated by officials.

Komsomolskaya Pravda, another organ, recently excerpted Alexander Rekemchuk's new book, a monograph in the *Lives of Great People* series designed for the Communist "Young Guard": "We know Scriabin better than we suppose." Rekemchuk points out that it was Scriabin's Fourth Symphony in C major Op. 54, the *Poem of Ecstasy*, which the All-Union Soviet Radio broadcasted into the "ether" as cosmonaut Yuri Gagarin made the world's first flight in outer space. And again, it was Scriabin's music which was played on 15 April, 1961 as the astronaut was welcomed triumphantly in Red Square. "We note that Scriabin's music more than any other is associated with days celebrating cosmonauts," he observes.

Scriabin's music not only celebrates astronauts in the

USSR, but invariably serves as incidental background to television, radio shows, and motion pictures which depict revolutionary events in Russia's history, particularly those of the fateful year 1905. Soviet composer Rodion Shchedrin (married to prima ballerina Maya Plissetskaya) says that he is always "surprised at how ideally" the history of the 1905 Revolution and Scriabin "coincide." The 1905 Revolution, it might be noted here, was a dress rehearsal for the Revolution of 1917. Official Tsarist statistics listed the casualties: 15,000 dead; 18,000 wounded; 79,000 imprisoned.

It is essential for Soviet ideology to see Scriabin as normal, but here the ground beneath us shakes. Neither Scriabin's putative madness, nor his patent eroticism may be examined. Only the progressive, healthy aspect of his music remains.

Controversy has always enveloped Scriabin. The music itself produces some of history's most extraordinary sounds, and today—when they are still astonishingly advanced—one can imagine the ear-shattering effect on listeners to these sonorous vapors and stratospheric lightning bolts underscored with agitated rhythms and overlaid with an intense musical message. The music itself caused, and causes, furor enough. But there is even less agreement about Scriabin's "meaning" than there was about his appearance as a person. Four different reminiscences, each written by a friend, disagree on so simple a matter as the color of Scriabin's eyes. Actually, they were hazel.

The two men closest to Scriabin both wrote biographies, Boris "de" Schloezer and Leonid Sabaneeff, and they contradict each other, particularly on the subjects of "sickly . . . unhealthy" and "madness." Schloezer, who first met the composer when he (Schloezer) was still a student of philosophy at Brussels University in 1902 and later became his brother-in-law, had a vested interest, and is vulnerable in his defense of the composer. "Schloezer was far from understanding Scriabin in everything," Delson writes. And indeed he was. For instance, Schloezer's statement, "The autonomy of Scriabin's creativity and its independence from all outside influences have always stunned me." Apart from the First Sonata and its personal tragedy, one can hear the contrasting happiness of his beginning second marriage in the *Poem of Ecstasy*, and later, the grief of World War I in the Preludes Op. 74.

Sabaneeff, whom Soviet critic Lev Danilevich dismisses as "pernicious and absurd," was the more brilliant writer. He also was closer to Scriabin at the end of the composer's lifetime when his music and thought became increasingly crucial. Sabaneeff, as we will see, sometimes is irresponsible, simply for the sake of a good metaphor or a salty phrase. But neither of these authorities can be denied his importance.

Schloezer contradicted Sabaneeff for calling Scriabin's musical colors "diseased," and for calling his eroticism "sexual," rather than, more respectably, sublimative ecstasy familiar to mystical saints. Both these scholars carried the feud with them when each went into exile in France, where each died unrepentant. Schloczer, keeper of the flame, wanted to protect Scriabin's reputation for the sake of his sister and their children. Sabaneeff, despoiler of the tomb, doubtless wanted to attract attention. In the West we incline to accept Sabaneeff over Schloezer. In Russia, neither serves: Schloezer because he emphasizes the high-flown irrationality of Scriabin's "idealistic philosophy" or mysticism; Sabaneeff because he hammers home negative aspects of Scriabin's personality such as insanity and excessive sexuality. To the Soviets both Schloezer with his heavy,

stultifying emphasis, and Sabaneeff with his harping ac-
cent, have "harmed the composer's memory."

Truth, in Scriabin's case, does lie in a well, and a bot-
tomless one at that. Perhaps biographical truth is much
like the truth of Gogol's poetic line that every school boy
in Russia memorizes: "Rare is the bird that can fly as far
as the middle of the Dnieper." He learns in his next class
that birds fly across oceans "vaster than any river by far."
But artistic truth is rarely diluted by natural history.

Sabaneeff in 1959 toward the last years of his life wrote
a long, introspective piece. In it he spoke of Scriabin's
"many hints at lust and utter depravity." He forthrightly
dates Scriabin's "psychosis" as beginning from the age of
thirty-five in 1906–7 and reveals how Alexander Brianchaninov, a wealthy magazine publisher, planned to send Scia-
bin to India to have him "consecrated by mahatmas."
Sabaneeff also reflects on that other facet—madness. He
decided that Scriabin was "clinically insane," either despite
or because of his genius. However, his evidence for this
allegation rests, flimsily enough, on Sabaneeff's having
shown Professor Serbsky, one of Russia's pioneer psychia-
trists—and for whom the present Serbsky Institute of Fo-
rensic Psychiatry in Moscow is named—a specimen of
Scriabin's handwriting. Dr. Serbsky noted that many of his
patients had a similar perfect and symmetrically lettered
script.

During Scriabin's lifetime, reviews of his concerts often
referred to him quite simply as decadent. "Being a decadent, Scriabin still tries to stand on his own feet . . . ,"
as the *New Times* of Moscow reviewed his 19 January,
1914 recital. He was called "cosmopolitan" as an epithet
of contempt, "Eurasian" for being a Slav and writing like
a Westerner, and un-Russian as the antithesis of what
patriotic nationalists wanted music to be. Scriabin himself

mocked Rachmaninov for writing a "Capriccio on Russian Themes" in order to be professionally "Russian" (and it is a poor piece of music, actually a Rhapsody).

But there was an opposing view about Scriabin even from the earliest. Nowhere is it better expressed than in the first piece of writing by Ossip Mandelshtam, the great poet still lamentably suppressed by the Soviet government. Writing during the Revolution of 1917, young Mandelshtam called Scriabin and Pushkin, "Two expressions of one sun; two expressions of one heart." The deaths of these two artists (both died prematurely—one at forty-three, the other at thirty-eight years of age), he asserted, "rallied the Russian people and ignited their sun above them. In these fateful hours of purification and storm, we raise Scriabin high overhead and his sun-heart burns us . . . To vanquish oblivion, even at the cost of death, that was Scriabin's motto, and that, the heroic striving of his art."

Under Stalin, not all Soviets saw Scriabin as sharing Pushkin's life-affirming sunniness. Nor did they respect Scriabin as "heroic." Anatol Lunacharsky, Russia's first Commissar of Education and a man without whose protective powers Soviet art would have been even more damaged than it was, saved Scriabin more than once. He himself in earlier years had tried to unite "revolution and religion," and so he sensed the pitfalls of that kind of intellectualism. In an article written in 1930, "The Significance of Scriabin in our Times," Lunacharsky emphasized that "Scriabin well understood the instability of the society in which he lived. . . . He felt the electricity in the air and reacted to its disturbance. In his music, we have the great gift of the Revolution's musical romanticism. . . ." All the while Lunacharsky eschewed Scriabin's mystical ideology, and he set the pattern of listening to the music and ignoring its intention.

Four years after that article, Lunacharsky died. By 1940 Scriabin was found guilty at a music Congress of "acute and morbid neuropathic egocentricity, totally un-Russian in his themes, and more anti-people than anything in the whole of Russian music." "Our bitterest enemy," Dmitri Shostakovich screamed. Yevgeni Zamyatin, a one-time Scriabin enthusiast,* now reminisced, "Scriabin's attenuatedly sensuous mysticism is no longer audible. This recent idol is quite forgotten."

Since the publication of Scriabin's complete letters in 1965, Russians definitely know that Scriabin carried on "flying" experiments with his wife, actually attempting to transport his body through the air. Some of his intimates had already recounted how Scriabin would say as they walked across a bridge, "I can fling myself over the railing and be suspended in air . . . unhurt, unharmed." Only one, Georgi Plekhanov, the Revolutionary leader, ever asked him to demonstrate.

In Scriabin's everyday walk he often "looked" as if he were flying, his friends pointed out. According to Margarita Morozova, his patron from 1903 to 1908, he loved to race along shady lanes far ahead and hop, skip, jump. This matched his temperament, which she defined as "the effort toward flight . . . He seemed to me like an elf or Shakespeare's Ariel, so lightly and high in the air did he leap." He also told friends that if he increased his speed, "and really wanted to," he could levitate. To the Fourth Sonata in F♯ Major Op. 30, Scriabin even wrote an accompanying poem describing a flight to a distant star which becomes a sun.

---

* In 1922 Zamyatin wrote a short story entitled "The Cave". In it, he depicts the end of the world and the cave into which he flees. He takes with him firewood, five potatoes, an ax, and Scriabin's last five Preludes Op. 74 as the collective last hope for his and for civilization's survival.

Despite this, in Soviet rationale Scriabin now is seen as a visionary artist foreguessing outerspace travel. His comments on how to play the second movement of the Fourth Sonata are cited as an anticipation of science's subsequent achievement. "I want this still faster," he said to a student, "as fast as possible, to the limit of possibility, so that it will be flight, the speed of light, straight to the sun, to the sun!"

Such "cosmic motifs" are no longer mystical, but materialistic realities in our era, the Soviets say. They ignore the climax of the Fourth Sonata poem, where Scriabin swallows the sun and becomes "My Self-of-Light." Even those famous bells which Scriabin wanted suspended from the clouds high over the Himalayas to summon the spectators and participants to his "Mysterium" are regarded by Soviets as a premonition of stereo and quadraphonic sound reception.

Einstein is invoked to support Scriabin's metaphysics as physics. After all, Einstein said, "There is always the element of poetry in scientific thinking. Natural science and natural music demand the same thought process." And certainly, the alertness and sharpness of Scriabin's mind, for all the haze of poetry and irrational abstractions we will see in Chapter VI, was acknowledged even by those most opposed to his concepts. Working toward opposite ends, perhaps Einstein and Scriabin started at the same place. *Sovetskaya Rossiya* is not really afield when it writes: "The soul of Scriabin the searcher is close to our own times—an era of wing-spreading scientific research, of deep experimentation in art."

It must be admitted that politically, Scriabin was never a reactionary, as were Claude Debussy and Richard Strauss, or Sergei Rachmaninov who first left Russia saying he "wouldn't take political instructions from my house-boy"

and who enjoyed telling faintly anti-Semitic stories. Scriabin welcomed the oncoming Revolution, and said so many
times. Socialism and his ideas frequently coincided, as
we will see when he moves from Russia to Switzerland
in 1904. But there are aspects of Scriabin's music which
make him incompatible with official Soviet sensibilities.
These are now ignored or rationalized out of existence.

Take the Tenth Sonata. Harold C. Schonberg describes
it as "a shudderingly sick piece, the sickest, I think, in the
history of music, but eternally fascinating." Scriabin used
to say that during the piece "the sun comes down and blis-
ters the earth." Soviet listeners hear it as a "nature piece"
and see its opening theme as a cuckoo bird call. Scriabin
does, indeed, describe "nature" in the Tenth. He referred
to the *allegro* main theme as "a sonata of insects . . ."—
insects being "kisses of the sun come to life." The Soviets
warn against Scriabinists who confuse the composer's person with the personality of the music.

The passionate interest Scriabin's music stirs in young
Russians has been well documented. Yevgeni Yevtushenko,
for instance, before his mastery was washed away by waves
of publicity, wrote a poem involving Scriabin, "Moscow
Freight Station." He describes a group of students who
work all night unloading watermelons freshly arrived from
the South. They do so in high spirits, as they are earning
enough money to buy a pair of tickets to an all-Scriabin
concert.

Pavchinsky in his book *Scriabin's Compositions of the
Late Period* (1969) talks about the *Poem of Ecstasy* in
this connection:

The "I Am" theme, along with the *Poem of Ecstasy* as a
whole, is an excellent example of innovation in its highest

sense, expressing a new quality, alloying many traditional elements, and embodying the leading ideas of the time. The *Poem of Ecstasy* can be set alongside the most outstanding works of Russian art composed in the atmosphere of the 1905 revolutionary upsurge. The idealistic "overlay" of the author's text need not disturb us. The "explanatory text" or commentary to the *Poem of Ecstasy* has long been forgotten. But a performance of this music invariably attracts a full hall of young people who have nothing in common with an idealistic [mystical] world view. They, nevertheless, feel an undeniable effect from the music with its unusual spirit. It is so close to young people with its affirmation of the essence of life as a process of struggle, of spiritual powers battling for everything that is new.

Young Russians seem to be searching for a link to their past. They are trying to correct Stalinist obliteration of the great turn-of-the-century world of intelligentsia. They accept Plekhanov's famous dictum, "Scriabin's music was his times expressed in sounds." In so doing, the young revel in still forbidden messages pretty much as they delight in old icons (as art works, of course, not religious objects). And perhaps it is the same with the now detoxified Scriabin music.

The authorities today have rendered Scriabin politically acceptable, although his esthetics were blind to matters of essential importance in any ideological government—class relationships, social reality, and morals themselves. Scriabin stands in diametric opposition to the fundamental Marxist platform that "Being determines Consciousness," or "Economics is Destiny." As a practicing mystic, Scriabin embodies the converse precept: "Consciousness determines Being."

Now, how to explain the resurgence of Scriabin's popu-

larity among young people in the West? It might be the
very mysticism eschewed by the Russians. These concepts
have been opened up through the languid dreams of mind-
expanding drugs and are now becoming widespread. Scriabin more than any other composer in music opened doors
of ecstasy. His friends called him "t e poet of ecstasy," and
he himself endured and enjoyed it more frequently, consistently, and with greater intensity, if we trust his secret
notebooks, than most others in mystical history. He tried to
communicate or share this inordin e sensation of bliss. As
Baudelaire (who found his paradis through drugs) said,
"Music excavates heaven," which is precisely what Scriabin
tried to do. He set as his goal the experience of art, not its
presentation.

Marina Scriabina, although she did not know her father
(she was four years old when he died), offers an explanation for Scriabin's presentday appeal to youth. In *The
Canada Music Book* (Autumn–Winter 1971) she says it is
based partly on "real affinities" and partly on "misunderstanding," and goes on to explain that Scriabin represents
"an attempt to escape the mediocrity of daily life . . . the
anguishing search for a spiritual life absent from the world
today." She also finds some of Scriabin's correspondences
in the quest for an art which "is not spectacle or diversion
but which wants to transform and magnify, to give the
fullness of joy and of life." And she adds ". . . without
forgetting the importance in Scriabin's thought of eroticism and even sexuality." She quotes her uncle, Boris
Schloezer, "In his dream of the end of the universe, Scriabin saw some kind of a grandiose sexual act."

Within the limits of space and time, Scriabin wanted to
explode man—all men—into a new universe. For a large
number of people today—no matter how divergent their
individual view of Scriabin as a man of ideas is, and to

those attuned to receive these special musical pulsations—
Scriabin has succeeded. For others, his music is like the
afternoon sun when the actinic rays have left, leaving heat
and light, but no fire to burn the flesh.

II Beginning Life

Some confusion exists regarding the accuracy of Scriabin's dates. Scriabin was born at 2:00 in the afternoon in Moscow on 25 December, 1871. Russians rather fancy a Christmas Day birth, so much so that Modest Tchaikovsky, much to historians' annoyance, falsified his brother's birthday. However, Scriabin actually was born then, as confirmed by official records.

At the time, Russia used the Julian calendar, established by Caesar in 46 B.C. As long ago as 1582, Pope Gregory adopted what became known as the Gregorian calendar—the one we use today in the West—which added ten days to the old calendar. By 1871, the Julian calendar was twelve days behind the Gregorian calendar, and so Christmas Day, December 25, at the time of Scriabin's birth fell in the West on January 6, or the time Russians celebrated Epiphany. Since March 1, 1900 the difference between the two calendars has expanded to thirteen days, and so from then until February 28, 2100, when there will be a fourteen-day variable, Scriabin's birthday and Christmas come on January 7. Christmas is celebrated by the Russian Orthodox Church in Soviet Russia and abroad on 7 January and not on January 6, the date it originally was in the nineteenth century. Lenin adopted the Gregorian calendar after the Revolution in an effort to align Russia with the West. Vital statistics for Russians born before 1918 are usually given in both "Old Style" and "New Style." Scriabin, for instance: 25 December, 1871/ 6 January, 1872.

Scriabin's death date, too, has been wrapped in a mystifying aura. Leonid Sabaneeff, although he was writing his *Reminiscences of Scriabin* as early as ten years after the composer's death, and was present at his bedside, stated that Scriabin died on Easter, doubtless to dramatize the messianic atmosphere. Scriabin in actuality died on 14 April (Old Style) or 27 April (New Style), 1915. Easter that year arrived early on 29 March/ 6 April. Even by stretching the weeklong festivities accompanying that holy day in Russia, Easter was more than two weeks over at the time of Scriabin's death. Sabaneeff also liked to say that Scriabin and Lenin shared the same birth year. This, too, was not true. Lenin was a year older than Scriabin, and the two men, in any event, never met. For those who wish to cling to mystical coincidence and who like omens, the two-and-a-half year lease on Scriabin's last apartment, now the State Scriabin Museum (11 Vakhtangov Street, Moscow, G-2), expired exactly on 14 April, 1915.

Scriabin was born into a noble but untitled family whose origins trace as far back as twelfth-century Central Russia. The family was predominantly military by profession—a general or two, a few colonels (Scriabin's grandfather was one, a tyrannical old man who ran his family like an Army platoon), and many captains.

Biographical psychologists are able to make much of Scriabin's childhood. He was an only child, motherless from the age of one. His mother had been a gifted pianist, a Little Gold Medalist at the St. Petersburg Conservatory —highest honors "for a woman." She was a pupil of Theodore Leschetizsky, quite possibly the greatest piano teacher of his century.

The widower father, Nikolai, spent all his time away from home in Moscow. He, contrary to his brothers and his father's wishes, entered the Foreign Service instead of the Army, and served throughout his lifetime in Turkey and Greece.* He died in 1914, a year before his son.

The care of the infant Scriabin was taken over by a doting aunt, Lyubov, who was twenty years of age when little Sasha was born, and her mother and sister, two *babushki*. His upbringing was by women exclusively, despite the presence in the house of seven uncles, senior to the child from twenty-five to six years in age. As carefully wrapped and reared in cotton wool as he was, Scriabin in later life referred to himself as a "glass child." He blamed the women—"grumpy lemon peels" is how he described his "mothers"—for his lifelong effeminacy of gesture and manner.

Lyubov's life began with her charge over the child, and her emotional life ended when he left the house at the late age of twenty-six to begin his own, independent life. At least physically, Lyubov survived her beloved ward and nephew by twenty-six years. From 1922, when the Scriabin Museum officially opened, until 1941 and the terrible war years, she served as caretaker. Lyubov's entire adulthood had been dedicated to her mother, her brothers, and to Scriabin. She remained a spinster all her life. Fortunately, she was not a clever woman, and little felt the hollowness of living her life vicariously through others.

---

* His signature validates Igor Stravinsky's first passport abroad in 1907.

None of the Scriabin family was very bright. Scriabin's own father and the older uncles were stiff, severe and rectitudinous. The younger men, in and out of the house on weekends and holidays from Army posts and cantonments, were "officer types," lightweight and out for nothing more than a good time. None of them understood anything of Scriabin the composer, certainly not his ideas, nor his personality, and naturally, never those "cathedrals of sound," as even Soviets call his music. The family, doubtless, was embarrassed by Scriabin's extravagance of thought and action, and by the appalling rumors which invariably circulated about him. Equally, they were puzzled by the wide public notice he always received, and the eternally devout and devoted adherents milling around him.

Scriabin found his father—of whom he saw more in his later years—boring, reactionary, and "absolutely dry of ideas." On one occasion he was constrained to write to his father bitterly, "You turn your family against me, instead of teaching them to read Russian art in my face." He nevertheless tried various rapprochements with his father in a ceaseless search for family harmony and unity, and they did reach the workable arrangement of meeting abroad for holidays. Even as a grown man Scriabin sometimes borrowed money from his father, only to repay it punctiliously.

No matter how oppressive it was for a child to grow up in a stilted world of old ladies, Scriabin retained a certain sense of happiness as a goal in life. This feeling for "life-joy," as the Russians call it, probably stemmed from his uncles who filled the house with laughter and music. Each played some musical instrument, though none well, and their visits contrasted strikingly to Sasha's loneliness. Scriabin could not have failed to draw currents of contentment, as well as masculinity, from them. If after long, Slavic travail in the habit of gloom, Scriabin was able to achieve a sense of joy in life, it was due to the uncles' imprinting. They even taught Scriabin how to dance, and though it left him as a pastime, it remained in his music, even as far advanced as in his late sonatas.

Whenever little Sasha was asked, "What school do you want to go to," he always answered fervently, "Only to the Cadet Corps." He always had shared a room with Dmitri, his youngest and favorite uncle. Sasha was desolate when Dmitri left to live as a cadet at the Second Moscow Cadet Corps in Lefortovo (now a KGB secret police prison) where the oldest uncle, a captain, had a spacious apartment. In 1882, as soon as he was eleven years old, he put on the sky-blue uniform with its silver epaulettes, like all good Scriabins, and moved into Lefortovo. The transition was slight in one way, because Lyubov and the *babushki* moved there with him.

The sickly, abnormally small boy (Scriabin would never grow taller than five-feet one-inch) was clearly out of place in the robustness of military tradition. The other cadets spotted this instantly. They resented even more the fact that this "accidental cadet" had come first out of the seventy applicants taking the entrance examination. He made no friends except one, Leonid Limontov, who later became an actor of some capability. The writer Alexander Kuprin, the only other future celebrity to emerge from Scriabin's class at the Cadet Corps, joined with the bullies in either ignoring or teasing little Scriabin.

Scriabin's "nerves" had already begun to show. His aunt took him periodically to the Therapeutic Clinic of Moscow University where he saw Dr. Grigori Zakharin, leading specialist in nervous disorders. Zakharin remained Scriabin's doctor for many years, although his only prescriptions for the psychic disturbances Scriabin suffered through were the "grape" or "water" cures—going South for the warm climate and the fresh fruit, or sea bathing in the Black Sea, and daylong drinking of fermented, slightly alcoholic mare's milk in various sanitoria of the South.

Scriabin had already displayed a talent for music. When he was three years old, he began begging Aunt Lyubov to sit down at the piano. By five years of age, he picked out pieces "softly and caressingly" with both hands. At eight, he fell in love, "not as a joke" according to Lyubov, and "composed" parts of an opera to be called "Lisa," after his sweetheart-playmate. The few scattered fragments that have been preserved through the years (by Lyubov, who took down the dictation) are the overture and the little second section Scriabin titled "Storm." They sound rather like Rossini's *William Tell*, the sort of music popular in Russia at that time.

When he was seven years of age, Scriabin's aunt had taken him from Moscow to St. Petersburg for an afternoon's "musical evaluation" by Anton Rubinstein, the greatest pianist of the era and head of the Petersburg Conservatory. The boy's gifts were abundantly present—a good ear (but not perfect pitch), fine finger reflexes, a quick rhythmic sense. Although Scriabin in later life detested Rubinstein's watery and flaccid compositions as superficial, artificial, and imported, Rubinstein's advice was wise, even if it went unheeded by the ambitious aunt: "Don't push the child . . . everything will come to him of its own accord."

Scriabin's serious music composition studies began in 1884–5 when he was twelve or thirteen. He studied with master contrapuntalist Sergei Taneyev, another of those composers unfairly neglected outside of Russian borders.

At this time Scriabin wrote his first real and complete composition, "Canon in D Minor," a prelude in hemiola—two's against three's—undulating, veiled, and full, if you look, of hints of future Scriabin. Two years earlier, he had studied piano with Georgi Konyus (Conus), a superb musician and later a well-known musical theorist.

Toward the end of Scriabin's first year at the Cadet Corps in 1883, there was a school gala at which Scriabin played some pieces he had picked up by ear from his father's second wife. For an encore, Scriabin played a little improvisation of his own. This constitutes his public début as a composer. The cadets were delighted at the unsuspected charm of their "hazel hen," Sasha. So, instead of putting ink in his bed and ducking him in the bath, they forced him to play dance tunes—waltzes and polkas—while they galloped around the Corps' rickety old upright piano. In this way, the Cadet Corps also contributed its dance element to Scriabin's music.

It was now evident that Scriabin would never be a soldier and that his musical talents were exceptional. He continued at the Corps, but twice a week took an hour's trip by horse-cart clear across Moscow to attend Nikolai Zveryev's "musical pension." Zveryev, Moscow's stellar piano teacher, adored the fourteen-year-old "Skryabushka," as he affectionately called him. He was also Russia's most talked about homosexual, except perhaps for Tchaikovsky, who visited Zveryev whenever he journeyed from St. Petersburg on business. Scriabin may have met Tchaikovsky at one of these times, although there is no record of this.

Scriabin already played the piano beautifully—"ethereally and fleetly." Zveryev was so enchanted with his new pupil he would summon the students who lived with him in the house to hear "Skryabushka" perform this piece or that—the Schumann Etudes on Paganini's Caprices, for example.

This doubtless irritated the adolescent Sergei Rachmaninov, a year Scriabin's junior and already unhappy, living as he was in that notorious teacher's house as a *pensionnaire* boarder. He could not have relished being shown how much more exquisitely Scriabin played than he. However, at that time Rachmaninov thought of himself as a composer not a pianist. Conversely, Scriabin was thought of solely as a pianist.

The impression of Scriabin as performer rather than creator persisted in Russian circles even when Scriabin's career could be seen in proper perspective. Igor Stravinsky, for instance, well after evidence pointed to the contrary, ascribed Scriabin's fame "more to his phenomenal abilities as a pianist than to whatever new qualities there were in his music."

Incidentally, Rachmaninov's extraordinary concert career, which so spurred the excellence of modern pianism all over the world, only came later . . . and, curiously enough, because of Scriabin. When Scriabin died he left his widow and children almost destitute. Rachmaninov, in honor of his old friend, toured Russia in a series of all-Scriabin programs. This was the first time, since Zveryev days, Rachmaninov had ever performed music other than his own. The event was also important in another way. Rachmaninov's playing, with its magnitude and grandeur, was diametrically different from Scriabin's. The Rachmaninov interpretations of Scriabin came so close after the composer's own renditions that they created a storm of protest among Scriabinists of 1915. Nevertheless, Rachmaninov revealed other possibilities of playing the music and, in a sense, broke Scriabin's monopoly on his own music. This will be discussed in more detail in Chapter XI.

Anyone looking at Scriabin's life cannot help but be dazzled by the brilliance of the personalities which surrounded him in the broad stream of Russian music. When he entered the Moscow Conservatory in 1887 at the age of sixteen (an unusually early age at that time), the spangled world of celebrity blazed even more lustrously. His precocious entry into the Conservatory had been arranged by Taneyev, and by Safonov.

Vassili Safonov was a man whose person and politics have been hotly argued. American critics describe him favorably; Soviet musicians lacerate him. His musicianship both as pianist and conductor was impeccable. He had been Leschetizsky's wonder-student in St. Petersburg. Now he was senior piano teacher at the Moscow Conservatory (later he would become its Director), teaching mostly at home where he had three grand pianos on different floors of his house. He outrageously spoiled his "Sashkina," giving Scriabin yet another and most unusual diminutive for "Alexander" or "Sasha."

Sixteen-year-old Scriabin, tiny and fragile as ever, delicate as a wristwatch mechanism that is always getting out of order from the slightest jar, and thirty-five-year-old Safonov, a gruff giant of a man towering over Scriabin and reeking of his Cossack heritage, made a startling pair. Sashkina's "touch" and "pedaling" became household words in the Safonov circle of pupils. On many occasions Safonov recalled that by the time Scriabin came to him there was nothing left to teach. Already he knew all there was to know, that is, "how to make the piano sound *not* like a piano."

Through Zveryev's pushing and Safonov's favoritism, Scriabin rather prematurely, according to fellow students, played a concert along with the "best" performers from the Conservatory at the Great Hall of Noblemen, now the Hall of Columns of Union House. He was seventeen at the

time, but played no compositions of his own. Next year on
10 December, 1888 at the Great Hall, he included his own
compositions in an otherwise conventional recital. That
date inaugurated his first official appearance as composer-
pianist.

Safonov knighted Scriabin as "Russia's Chopin." He
meant this as an accolade, but the world took the phrase
and used it pejoratively to mean "derived, unoriginal, copy-
catting." Much has been written about the similarity between Chopin's music and Scriabin's. But today's listeners
have only to hear, say, the piano and orchestra Fantasy in
A Minor, posthumously orchestrated by G. Zinger, to know
how un-Chopinesque Scriabin already was at seventeen,
and more importantly how individually Russian he sounds.

During the Conservatory years and after, there was an
ever deepening intimacy between "rough and despotic"
Safonov and his gentle, lacelike pupil. They drank together
at hotels. They exchanged poems. Safonov one night composed a rhyming acrostic on Scriabin's name, written as if
he were Scriabin himself and insightful of the future:

> Strong a creator's sight
> Carries all to heaven's heights
> Radiant sound of sweetest light
> I a fountain of delight
> All life's plan
> By man is won
> In the end, I am,
> No doubt a holy man.

Scriabin wrote a poem for his "Vassiliyaevich." It goes
to the effect (in the translation of Maria Safonoff, the
daughter who now lives in New York City): "Our maestro

glorious/ Of Russian leaders none is more than he/ Blessed
with creative ardor/ None as free to steer the great orchestral flow harmonious . . ."

Safonov conducted the New York Philharmonic from
1906 to 1909 with great distinction. He had temporarily
left Russia after the 1905 Revolution, during which he stub-
bornly railed against strikers and agitators. In his own
sphere at the Conservatory he highhandedly repressed student demonstrations of Revolutionist sympathy. In America, Safonov was the first conductor to dispense with the
bâton, to wear formal evening dress even for afternoon
concerts ("Music must be honored at all times"), and to
introduce Scriabin's music to the American public.

Anton Arensky, another teacher at the Moscow Conservatory, detested Scriabin. To his discredit in history he failed
Scriabin in composition, of all things, although he was
manifestly the most gifted, inspired and facile of young
talents at the time.

The Scriabin-Arensky feud fueled the engines of scandal
in its day. Since then, it has been much mooted. The consensus of eyewitnesses and subsequent reflections as to the
pros and cons show that Scriabin was too "original" for the
limited imagination of "petty" Arensky. Arensky was a
strange man, drunken, debauched, flighty and unpredict-
ably irascible. He suffered from having too much talent
unsupported by genius. But he got along well with his
other students who were less intractable—Rachmaninov
and later, Alexander Grechaninov.

The open rift occurred when Arensky assigned the composition class "an orchestral scherzo." Scriabin turned up
with an overture to an opera he thought he might write.
Arensky, standing on protocol and insisting on his profes-
sorial prerogatives (although he was not ten years older
than his pupil), forced a scherzo from him. However,

Scriabin refused to accept Arensky's corrections and "improvements" on the scherzo, and prevented the Conservatory orchestra from playing it. (Scriabin's adamancy over orchestration was repeated when Rimsky-Korsakov tried to reorchestrate the Concerto in F♯ Minor Op. 20, as he had doctored Mussorgsky's *Boris Godunov*. Scriabin simply disallowed Rimsky's suggestions, and the instrumentation we hear today is almost completely Scriabin's own.)

Scriabin's cohorts at the Conservatory called him "Pussy," because of his femininity, and Scriabin did not seem to mind. It was an incredibly distinguished group of fellow students—Bronislaw Huberman, the violinist; Modest Altschuler, then a cellist with his own trio, and subsequently a conductor of Russian music concerts in New York; Josef Lhevinne, who could play the piano faster than anyone else, as Americans had occasion to hear during his concert tours and long professorship at the Juilliard School.

Alexander Goldenveizer was another junior pupil at the Conservatory. He later headed the piano department until his death in 1961. Goldenveizer introduced Leo Tolstoi to Scriabin's music and Tolstoi called it "sincere . . . genius," which was tantamount in pre-Revolutionary Russia to being blessed by the Pope. Even throughout the troubled years of Stalinism, Goldenveizer used all his formidable prestige as senior pianist and pedagogue to defend and espouse Scriabin's music. He had been the first to play the Fantasy in B Minor Op. 28, although musically it does not represent any high-water mark from a Scriabinic gauge. He was among the earliest exponents of the piano role in the quasi-concerto, *Prometheus*. Time has justified Goldenveizer's consistency, and his regard for Scriabin went far beyond the sentiment of good old days at school or personal loyalties.

There was also one young girl at the Conservatory in

Scriabin's time, Elisabeth Kashperova. She is of interest to
us today because her nephew Alexei became the musicologist and editor-annotator of the thousand letters Scriabin
wrote in the course of his lifetime. (Another estimated
four hundred have proved untraceable.) "So much untruth
has been written about Scriabin," Kashperov said in a letter shortly before his death in 1970, "I have tilled un-
ploughed soil of virgin lands." Kashperov's service to the
Scriabin cause has been without equal. His compilation
of all the letters ever written to Scriabin, titled *Annals in
the Life and Creative Work of Scriabin* has been completed by another Scriabinist, Professor G. Bernandt, with
the assistance of the Central Museum of Musical Culture.

Tragically, a fierce competitive streak developed during
Scriabin's Conservatory years. When emergent star Semeon
Samuelson said that he was learning all forty-eight Preludes
and Fugues of Bach's *Well-Tempered Clavier,* Scriabin
announced he was "readying" all thirty-two Beethoven
Sonatas. He also pounded away at Balakirev's "Islamey"
and Liszt's finger-breaking "Fantasy" on Mozart's opera,
Don Giovanni. The year was 1891, and it was a climactic
one. Scriabin overpracticed, severely straining his right
hand. Doctor Zakharin said that he would have to abandon
any hope of a virtuoso career. Scriabin described the mis-
hap in his notebook as "The most serious event of my
life," and he moaned about fate destroying his "goals of
fame and glory." Scriabin suffered periodically for the rest
of his life with pain in his right hand, and the loss in keyboard volume and mastery it entailed.

However, he put his sorrow to good use. He composed
his first masterpiece of major proportion, the First Sonata
in F Minor Op. 6 with all its overwhelming tragedy and
"Funeral March." He also conceived at this time of writing

music for the left hand alone. Not until 1894, when he was
twenty-two, did he actually compose the famous Prelude
and Nocturne Op. 9 for the left hand, and these pieces
with their astonishing delicacy have become in our minds
Scriabin's early signature.

In 1895 he played the Prelude and Nocturne publicly for
the first time at a recital of his own compositions in the
house of the Sabashnikovs, millionaire art patrons and
publishers. When you consider how for so many years
Scriabin's name was synonymous with these left-hand tricks
of virtuosity and beauty, how in America in 1906 when
Scriabin arrived for a concert tour he was billed as "the
left-handed Chopin" (Lhevinne had introduced the pieces
earlier that year in his American début), and how photog-
raphers frequently photographed his left hand as a publicity stunt, it is amusing to read Morozova's account of the
pieces' première performance. The drawing room was full
of people, she says, but they were "puzzled" by the music,
"applauded very weakly," and many guests "fled."

During his Conservatory years, Scriabin tried to leave
the apartment Aunt Lyubov and the *babushki* had taken
near the school. He moved in with some friends, musical
buddies really. He was miserable, and Lyubov came and
collected him, according to her version of the story.

Scriabin also fell in love, again seriously and "not as a
joke," with Natalya Sekerina. In 1891 she was fifteen years
old, five years his junior. A pattern of taste for very young
girls and for much older, taller men ripples throughout
Scriabin's life. It is hard to know which was really more
painful to Scriabin, the catastrophic hand injury or the un-
successful, unconsummated affair with Natalya. At one
point he wrote, "Listen to this voice of a sick and tor-
mented soul. Remember and pray for the man whose en-

tire happiness is yours and whose entire life belongs to you!" She didn't.

It was for Natalya that Scriabin wrote his only song. (He also composed another for Florence Scarborough, an American operatic soprano living in Paris in 1904 who was very friendly with Scriabin, but it has never been located.) Scriabin's words to the Natalya song are replete with premonitions of his later "philosophy." He tells her that by the power of the mind he can enter her soul, and that this idea of "creativity" will reveal to her a "universe of delight."

Scriabin wrote Natalya fifty-six letters, one of the rare long correspondences he sustained. They contain arresting passages revealing a young Russian of that day growing up in mind, body, soul and experience. Many of the letters are the peacock preening of a young man in love, but glimpses of his inner world also flicker throughout. As in his private notebooks, we read the development of his idea that "creativity" is the source of all human power, that people "can expect nothing from life except that which they create by themselves alone." Embittered by the hand injury and life's unfairness, he turned away from God, usurping His creative position of omnipotence for himself, as we will see in greater detail in Chapter VI.

The trick of Scriabin's mind was to convert life's eternal tragedy into personal inner bliss. Once, as early as June 1893, he wrote Natalya what later would become something of a life theme for him: "The star is so beautiful, and I so love my star that if I cannot gaze on it, if it cannot shine down on me in my life, and if I cannot fly to it, then thought perishes, and with it everything else. Better that I disappear in mad flight toward her. So the idea will remain, and that will triumph."

Scriabin graduated from the Conservatory in 1892, but only with the Little Gold Medal. For the Great Gold Medal, which Rachmaninov received, he would have had to have honors in both piano and composition. Arensky, alone among the Conservatory staff of teachers, spitefully declined signing Scriabin's graduation diploma. Although biographers have wanted to present Scriabin as victorious over his piano nemesis, he did not play the Mozart-Liszt Fantasy at his graduation recital. His program only included Bach's "Capriccio on the Departure of a Beloved Brother," Beethoven's Sonata Op. 109, Chopin's Ballade in F Major, a trivial Waltz by Liapunov, and the Schumann-Liszt "Spring Night."

After leaving the Conservatory and for the next several years, Scriabin's life consisted of "socializing," as he called it. He played private concerts in the mansions of maecenases. He met Josef Hofmann. Hofmann had been a child performer and, unlike many buds which are forced to bloom too early, he continued his prodigious career. He was friendly with Scriabin, and strongly influenced by his pianism when they met in 1896. Their meetings were always amicable, though occasionally filled with rivalry. Hofmann nearly took Natalya away from Scriabin.

Scriabin liked to stay up all night talking ideas with friends. He also drank himself into oblivion. Safonov said of Scriabin in those years that he drank so much, "he was drunk for the rest of his life." The adult Scriabin of later years has often been described as having a look of "drunkenness," and this expression in his eyes has been captured in a few photographs and in one of Pasternak's drawings of 1909. Scriabin wanted "drunkenness" in music, and some of his later pieces are so marked. But he regarded alcoholic intoxication as a "coarse and physical" intimation of a

more sublime spiritual ecstasy. The drunkenness of his eyes
and in his expression was actually an absenting of himself
from the outer world of reality.

Except for an occasional lapse in Switzerland in 1905
or a bout or two in 1911, the more Scriabin's inner world
progressed, the less he depended on alcohol. Soon he would
renounce it altogether, except for a glass of champagne
before going on the concert stage, and a few more glasses at
post-recital celebrations. But in his era of socializing after
the Conservatory years, his nervous attacks, exacerbated by
alcohol, grew frightening. Aunt Lyubov, thinking she describes the birth of a musical composition, tells how he
moaned at night, saw visions, trembled and shivered in alternately hot and cold sweats, and lay exhausted all the
next day until evening. In between these periods of agony,
Scriabin soared, maniacally perhaps, and he did compose
marvelously. The twelve resplendent Etudes Op. 8 belong
to this post-Conservatory period.

Scriabin began to grow his beard and mustaches which
had first sprouted only with difficulty. He trained them "of-
ficer-like," and the military look of his face wreathed in
hair never jibed with his fussy, fidgety demeanor and physical delicacy. His hands were small (which is why he never
played in public his handstretching Etude in major ninths,
Op. 65 No. 1), very white, unveined, padded with smooth
flesh and scarcely wrinkled even at the knuckles.

Here is Sabaneeff discussing Scriabin's appearance. Their
acquaintance first dates from this socializing period.

If it is possible to define the personality of Scriabin as
seized by some kind of an electrical awakening, as something luminous and joyous, it would still be necessary to
say at the same time that he had no "grandeur of spirit." He
attracted, but he did not impose, not in the slightest. This

fearfully restless, minute man lacked the power which inner
psychic muscles give, which Wagner, for instance, that no
less active and expansive man, had.

Of course, the matter does not rest in their nervousness
or their small stature. (Wagner was even shorter than Scriabin.) It is something else, something that shines through
their work. Scriabin lacked *power*, but he had a burning,
blinding, unearthly joy. Moreover, Scriabin did not need nor
understand power. It was foreign to him. His exterior and his
psyche were in strange harmony with his half-childish caprices which showed in his quick changes of mood, his
sudden drop in spirits, and his fear of infection and bacteria.
His delicacy and refinement were the product of his early
pampering and advantages. He was undoubtedly "a bug on
cleanliness," as he called himself. There was not the faintest
touch of slovenliness about him . . .

But no matter how he took care of his appearance, he still
wasn't looked at in society. He did not attract attention by
his appearance. He was small, plain, unnoticeable in a crowd,
drew no stares to him. This made all his personal work on
himself all the stranger, almost comical. It seemed a power-
less labor leading to no results. I have not yet mentioned how
the external appearance which he chose for himself agreed
so little with him. . . .

And Sabaneeff goes on to speak of the mustaches which
Scriabin brushed "wickedly upward on concert days," and
how his brother thought he looked vaguely like a cock-
roach. His hair, which had been blond in his youth, turned
reddish brown with age.

Boleslav Yavorsky, who later declined meeting Scriabin
privately, contributes a memoir as to how young Scriabin
appeared. He was very "controlled and correct in manner,
reminiscent of his Cadet Corps training . . . clever looking . . . lively . . . with a high, clear, flexible tenor voice,

very pleasant in timbre . . . hands always in motion . . .
enchanting play in the eyes."

In 1894, Scriabin met Mitrofan Belaieff, the St. Petersburg publisher who came to love him. Belaieff enjoyed
parties as much as Scriabin did at that time. He had refused to join his family's enormous timber enterprises, preferring to play second violin at his "String Evenings" in his
house in St. Petersburg. All the Russian music world attended, and guests enjoyed the lavishness of new music,
good food and more than abundant drink. Tchaikovsky had
just died, to Belaieff's regret, but not Scriabin's; still there
were other powerful figures in Belaieff's circle to join in his
support of young Scriabin. César Cui, whose fame rests on
his having been a member of the Mighty Fistful, the pioneer composers who created the Russian nationalist school;
Alexander Glazunov, whom Belaieff discovered when he
was still a high school student; Anatol Liadov, whose pleasant enough music is still occasionally heard, and Rimsky-
Korsakoff, whose greatness we acknowledge more and more
today. Nearly all these musicians had jobs other than
music, for Russian music had only begun to move from its
amateur status into professionalism. This vital move was to
a great extent made possible by Belaieff's patronage.

The Scriabin-Belaieff friendship was one of the closest
either man had ever known. Again, it was marked by dis-
parity in age and physique. Belaieff was thirty-five years
older than Scriabin (Safonov, through whose offices the
two met, was twenty years older than Scriabin), and
Belaieff, like Safonov, looked twice Scriabin's height.
Belaieff instantly agreed to publish Scriabin's music, paying
him the equivalent of $100 for a sonata and $25 for a prelude, high fees indeed for an unknown. But Belaieff knew
how to pick swans, and rarely did they turn out to be
geese.

Belaieff presented Scriabin personally in recitals in St. Petersburg and Moscow, gave him expensive gifts—a grand piano, fancy luggage, a bound first edition of Chopin's works—and guaranteed him a stipend of $50 a month, ostensibly to be applied as payments for future compositions. This flow of patronage was never quite repaid however. In fact, Scriabin was perpetually in Belaieff's debt, and Belaieff was forever advancing him higher and higher amounts of money. Neither man minded, for Belaieff was generous, and Scriabin unconscionable. Belaieff also subsidized the annual Glinka Prize for the best Russian composition of the year. Scriabin consistently won, and the Prize's $500 honorarium supplemented his yearly "pension."

In June, 1895, Belaieff sent Scriabin on his first trip abroad to Germany, for travel experience and to see his father, who with his new family had grown less and less inclined to visit Russia at all. Having become accustomed to the servility of the conquered people of the foreign countries in which he served, Nikolai felt that the pleasing conventions of tradition had left Russia, and so preferred to holiday in more civilized Europe.

Actually, Belaieff was alarmed at Scriabin's self-torturing nervousness and was sending him to Dr. Wilhelm Erb, Europe's most renowned neuropathologist, then teaching and practicing at Heidelberg University. This was Scriabin's first contact with then-nascent psychiatry. He felt instant relief. For a while after Dr. Erb's talk treatment, Scriabin's fierce migraine headaches, which had pinned him under their pain, disappeared. Later, through Scriabin's own efforts, they would vanish entirely. After thirty years of age, Scriabin rarely knew sickness or physical suffering until the very end, thirteen years later.

In the autumn of 1895, Belaieff and Scriabin toured Europe together. Gigantic Belaieff sat on stage while minuscule Scriabin played. Belaieff introduced him to French personalities, including the "decadents," who defined France's *fin de siècle* literary and musical coteries. At that time, Paris was a city of "ephebes and opium," where "suicide by hallucination," took place. Paris was rife with drugs and homosexuality as established by Baudelaire, Verlaine and Mallarmé to be succeeded by Jean Cocteau and André Gide.

Belaieff hated being outside the borders of Russia so he returned early. Scriabin remained for a few months, continuously sending him travel postcards of music, notably the twenty-four Preludes Op. 11 which were primarily descriptions of Scriabin's journey to the West. As the music tells our ears, he sees everything with Russian eyes. He paints a picture of the Heidelberg Castle, of a torrential stream as it crashes on the rocks working its way to the river and then the sea, of the loneliness he feels at being abroad. Scriabin promised Belaieff that he would send him forty-eight preludes as his task for the 1895 year. He sent twenty-four, and next year completed all save one (making a total of forty-seven) which appeared as Preludes Op. 13, 15, 16 and 17.

Scriabin wrote Belaieff one hundred eighty-four letters over the period from 1894 to 1903, when Belaieff died. The letters are sparsely interesting. They mainly consist of requests for extra money, excuses for carelessness about reading proofs, and deceptions as to whether he has actually sent off a composition on time or not. Belaieff's letters to Scriabin, which Scriabin never bothered to save for posterity (his first wife later saved some of them), are full of reproach and recrimination. "What do you mean when you put a staccato dot on a note and then tie it to the next?" And he reproves him for laziness, dilatoriness, irresponsibility. He makes Scriabin submit expense accounts. "Answer yes or no, and don't be a Muscovite," he snaps at one point. "You've had that piece long enough! Send it to me right away." He was speaking of the Second Sonata which took Scriabin six years of fussing before he released it.

Soviet commentators on the Scriabin-Belaieff correspondence are harsh on the patron. Matthew Pressman, a classmate of Scriabin's at the Conservatory, writing in retrospect long after Scriabin's death said, "The extraordinarily refined, sensitive and effeminate Scriabin suffered under Belaieff's mentorship. Belaieff loved him and helped him materially, yes, but he treated him badly."

Valentin Asmus, the distinguished professor of philosophy at Moscow University and a Scriabinist who actually heard Scriabin play one of his last recitals, writes in his introduction to Scriabin's letters (edited by Alexei Kashperov): "In Scriabin's youth Belaieff reproved him for being precipitous and insufficiently modest in wanting to compose, as he put it, 'a ninth symphony.' Belaieff never suspected how close he came in his reproaches to cutting down the heights of Scriabin's aims . . ."

These judgments are too harsh. Without Belaieff badgering Scriabin to send more and more compositions, there would ultimately have been less music. Scriabin never wrote "on demand," as Mozart did, nor would he ever be pressured to write at the dinner table like Vivaldi. (He did write some of his letters standing up in a train station with gloves on.) Nor would he be Bach-like and write a piece for violin, next month letting it turn up for four harpsichords according to occasion and necessity.

Without Belaieff's constant, benevolent and cautious guidance, Scriabin's life would have been more disordered than it already was. Much of the maturity which Scriabin surprisingly shows in later life emanates from the disciplines, hurtful as they may have been, Belaieff imposed as consistently and tenderly as possible on his favorite protégé among protégés.

Indeed, Belaieff's advice was unusually sound. He counseled against Scriabin's marriage in 1897 to Vera Issakovich, a Karaim Jewess converted to Russian Orthodoxy (a common practice in Tsarist, anti-Semitic Russia). Everybody was against the marriage, particularly Lyubov who didn't like the girl. But Scriabin was headstrong. Twenty-six was the age when men should "settle down" and, besides, he was a man with a Concerto already behind him. He instantly regretted his marriage. No sooner had the train left the platform, leaving a weeping Lyubov amid all the rejoicing relatives, than Scriabin looked at Vera and "knew" he had made a terrible mistake. He continued to regret the mistake for the rest of his life, even after the couple irreconcilably parted company in 1904.

Vera was likable enough and an excellent pianist, as evidenced by the fact that she later taught at both the Moscow and Petrograd Conservatories. Unusually, she was a mere four years younger than Scribian (his second wife-mistress would be twelve years younger), but she was brunette, with big, black, sad eyes, dark like his father's wife, Olga Fernandez.*

Vera was headstrong, tight-fisted and tight-minded, totally unsuited to Scriabin's temperament and, logically enough, unable to follow him in his fanciful flights toward stars and suns. In May, 1898 the couple returned from a long honeymoon in Paris. Vera was pregnant and had complained the whole time. Scriabin composed his tragic-heroic Third Sonata in F♯ Minor Op. 23, the last of his romanti-

---

* Olga Fernandez's origins were obscure. Nikolai told his family that she was of "Italian" descent. She, like the first wife, also played the piano.

cally thunderous, emotionally agonizing, "psychological" works.

Divorce was a serious matter in pre-war Russia, and Vera stoutly refused ever to cancel the vows taken in the Russian Orthodox cathedral of her father's home-town, Nizhny-Novgorod (now Gorki). Even after Scriabin began living openly with Tatyana Fyodorovna Schloezer in 1905, Vera continued to give Scriabin recitals, to his chagrin, until her death in 1920. In those early days, she was one of the few to perform all-Scriabin programs in concert. The eight Etudes Op. 42 were the last pieces of music she actually studied with her husband, but she played the more advanced and mysterious music as far as the Sixth Sonata Op. 62. In 1916, after the composer's death, she and of all people Safonov gave the first performance of *Prometheus, The Poem of Fire* Op. 60. By this time Safonov had been both musically and, because of Vera, personally estranged from Scriabin.

Scriabin was a husband and father in 1898, and the family's expenses had become heavier.* Friends stepped in to help. Safonov had become head of the Moscow Conservatory, and fortunately for his machinations, Paul Schloezer, one of the piano professors and uncle of the next Mme. Scriabina had died, leaving a vacancy on the staff. Safonov proposed Scriabin for the professorship. Scriabin's duties were light, in order to leave him free time to compose. But he ended up with nearly two dozen pupils, and had to listen to student recital examinations for nine hours nonstop at each semester's end.

Scriabin asked for Belaieff's advice. He replied: "You

---

* Altogether, Vera would bear three girls and a boy. The eldest died as a direct result, it would seem, of the tension in the Scriabin household created by the parents' quarreling over divorce. However, the boy died later, at age eight, from a less psychosomatic illness—fever.

know full well I have always been for a definite occupation
to train a person to regularity and a sense of responsibility.
But what about your health? Are you physically strong
enough?" Within a year of accepting the professorship,
Scriabin wrote Belaieff, "The conservatory, of course, inter-
feres with my working, mainly because it disrupts my con-
centration. You have to listen to too much music by other
people." This shows in some of his "Conservatory" music.

The idea of Scriabin as teacher does not fit well with the
idea of Scriabin as composer of self-consuming dreams. His
nature militated against teaching; it bored him dreadfully.
His fellow professors resented him not only as the Director's pet, but also for being so young, and much has been
written about how bad a teacher he was. But this is contradicted by the passionate testimonies his students have left.
He was extraordinarily conscientious. He began Maria
Nemenova-Lunz, for example, with the basic hand position, scales, and arpeggios—all the tedious mechanics of
pianism which Conservatory professors usually delegate to
assistants. Nemenova-Lunz summarized her satisfactory ap-
prenticeship with Scriabin as, "He summoned from me
everything of which I was capable."

Morozova, who studied privately with him, explains that
"He burned with too much creative fire," but he was "absolutely exceptional as a teacher. He could completely en-
chant a student with music and playing, make him forget
his own mood and plunge into work driving himself toward perfection." Morozova also substantiates what many
others of his contemporaries said about Scriabin. He felt
that all art before Beethoven was "dead," that all new art
stemmed from Beethoven, but he detested him anyway,
and only liked Chopin's "lyricism," Liszt's "magical sonorities," and Wagner as a "personality." He spurned Tchaikovsky ("He makes me ill," Scriabin said), and as for his

contemporaries, "He never spoke of them. It was as if they did not exist for him."

In fact, in all of Scriabin's correspondence, there are remarkably few references to compositions by other composers alive at Scriabin's time. He asked Belaieff in a letter of 1897 how Rachmaninov's First Symphony had been "received" when Glazunov conducted its first performance. In 1905, in an otherwise totally businesslike letter to Glazunov (who later co-headed Belaieff's publishing house with Rimsky after the patron's death), Scriabin asks how he is and what he's writing, out of automatic courtesy. Scriabin did write about dead composers, and rarely then, too. "Oh, how bored I was at the concert listening to all that music by Beethoven, Brahms and Mendelssohn!" he says to Tatyana Fyodorovna Schloezer-Scriabina in 1908.

Nevertheless, he taught his students compositions by many composers, and they played them well. Perhaps some of Scriabin's own arhythmical idiosyncrasies rubbed off on them. Perhaps they didn't play digitally so fast and so loudly in the school of "shattering pianism" as some of the other Conservatory students. Excellent teachers do not necessarily produce stars every time, but the students were brilliant, and recognizably so. They were also bound to him as if by sorcery.

Once, Scriabin refused to teach Morozova and cancelled her lessons, because she was insufficiently "serious." They were talking during intermission at the Bolshoi Theater, and he did not notice her tears. When he learned, finally, that her husband had died and it had been a terrible year for her, he resumed the lessons free of charge. "That way I can feel free myself," he said.

In 1899, Scriabin was invited by Paul de Conne to teach at the prestigious Vienna Conservatory. De Conne had written his superiors after an inspection of the Moscow

Conservatory, "I almost think Scriabin is the best professor they have." Scriabin declined, because teaching abroad would drain his energies even more than at home.

Scriabin managed a surprising amount of creative work during his four-year tenure as professor. In 1898 he composed *Rêverie* in E minor Op. 24, an exquisite, transparent little prelude lasting about three minutes and requiring a full orchestra. Rimsky-Korsakov conducted its first performance and the success was such that he had to encore it. Next year in 1899, Scriabin composed an Andante for Strings in F Major, as yet unpublished, and nine Mazurkas Op. 25, which show an enlargement of scope and emotional deepening when compared to the lightness and vapidity of his youthful Ten Mazurkas Op. 3.

He also began his massive First Symphony with chorus (Belaieff's "Ninth" Symphony) which he completed in 1900, along with the grand Fantasy.* The Fantasy is big pianistically, and a great favorite of virtuosi—it shows the result of having heard "too much music of other people." Additionally, there are two preludes Op. 27, very popular with Soviet pianists, and a Second Symphony in C Minor Op. 29, all finished in publishable form in 1901. For four summers—since winters were consumed by the students at the Conservatory—this output is not at all bad. As music, however, the pieces are not entirely real Scriabin, not the Scriabin to come as soon as he liberated himself from teaching. There is a certain mustiness, uncharacteristic of either earlier or later Scriabin.†

Scriabin's unique attempt at opera—the first music form to fascinate him when he was taken as a child to the Bolshoi—also belongs to these Conservatory years. In 1900 he planned the idea, and spent two years intermittently writ-

---

* See Chapter II, page 31.
† See Chapter X, page 184.

ing the libertto in rhymed and metrical stanzas. The hero
is Scriabin himself, a nameless "philosopher-musician-
poet." "I AM THE MAGICIAN OF A POWERFUL
HEAVENLY HARMONY, lavishing caressing dreams on
mankind," he sings. "With the POWER OF LOVE I will
make life's springtime. I will find long-desired peace BY
THE STRENGTH OF MY WISDOM." (Scriabin's capi-
tal letters.) There are scenes in magical gardens, and a
grand ball at the palace where the princess wearies of fawn-
ing flatterers. In the end the hero wins the princess ("I will
exhaust you with my overpowering kisses, now you will
learn sweet felicity!"). The hero leads a people's rebel-
lion and releases all the prisoners jailed by the king. The
philosopher-musician-poet and his princess die in each
other's arms, in ecstatic, culminative bliss, the "Act of the
Last Attainment." "I am the apotheosis of world creation.
I am the aim of aims, the end of ends," announces the
hero, to no one's surprise by this time.

The text of the opera, although quite incomplete, was
published after Scriabin's death. Much of it reflects the
Socialist theories then current in Russia. The Cupid and
Psyche halo of Greek mythology made the text culturally
reputable, but the mystical climax removes the work from
any Marxist acceptability. Snippets of its music—"What's
that new thing you're playing?" friends asked; "It's from
my opera," he answered—became independent pieces, published separately as piano poems and preludes, clearly ora-
torical and declamatory in style. The Poem Op. 32 No. 2
in D Major and the "Tragic Poem" in B Flat Major Op. 34
are two such pieces. Perhaps it is à propos here to note
that while Scriabin was wrestling with his opera, Debussy
produced *Pelléas et Mélisande*, although Scriabin would
not have a chance to hear that work until 1907.

Scriabin attained his goal of fame, all right, in March,

1902. His friends the Monighetti sisters (daughters of the doctor who attended the Cadet Corps, and most affectionate admirers of their mutual Sasha) underwrote expenses for the first all-Scriabin orchestral and piano program. Safonov conducted the *Rêverie* and First Symphony. Scriabin played the Third Sonata and a whole list of preludes, mazurkas, and his Polonaise in B Flat Minor Op. 21. He had composed the Polonaise because he needed a "big piece" to pad a recital given in Paris on his honeymoon.

The year 1902 was a void, however, in Scriabin's composing calendar, and the first extended period in his life during which he wrote nothing. (1910 was the second and only other time.) He hated to force music unwillingly from within himself, to "invent" it—*pridumyvat'*, as he called it—or to "obtain by tormenting," *vymuchivat'*. He expected music to arrive spontaneously, although it did not always do so, emanating as he thought it did from some source within himself. He would ultimately call this source his "HE," as if his soul were inhabited by someone else, an even mightier creator.

Once in 1896 in a letter to Belaieff concerning the Preludes Op. 11, he dug in to resist Belaieff's pressure. Here he makes the only reference in all his letters to the difference between creative and technical composing. "Of course I could write the four missing pieces today, that is, I could *devise* them, which I would have to do, since I haven't the faintest inclination to compose. But I really don't want to do that, as none of the other pieces are invented. Yet, when I say this, you won't believe that I am *tired* of composing. I simply have to have a month or so without any composing at all, and not force at all."

So, the year 1902 was not simply a silence after all. It was a fallow gathering of energy in the force field of Scriabin's genius. When he resumed composing in 1903, he gave the world a spurt of his finest creations. He began writing those iridescent, whirling veils of resonances which would become his trademark. Never again would he write so much, nor so frantically in so short a period of time.

III   Middle Years

Scriabin's various neuroses manifested themselves increasingly in obvious ways, but he was spared one common symptom—the inability to make decisions. He always knew what he wanted and usually fumed and maneuvered until his wishes came to fruition. In 1903, he had passed the age of thirty and had written his Op. 30—the Fourth Sonata which has proved to be instantly agreeable and persuasive to audiences. (The Fourth Sonata was apparently drafted in its entirety in two days; however, one school claims he held it back for two years until he perfected its "finishing touches." Although there is no proof for this contention, it would advance the beginning of Scriabin's middle period of composing style to 1902.)

Never was the clarity of Scriabin's mind more evident than in 1903. It was a year for definite action, and decisions poured from him. He resigned from the Conservatory.* He abandoned his opera without so much as an

* The year before, he had threatened to quit if his favorite pupil Alexander Horowitz (uncle of the pianist Vladimir) was not awarded the Gold Medal, which he deserved but did not receive. The prize was split between two other Scriabin students, Nemenova-Lunz and another woman.

50

afterthought. He composed an unprecedented stream of music—thirty-six pieces in all, from Op. 30 to Op. 43, the hour-long Third Symphony in C Major (according to Kashperov) or C Minor (according to Mikhailov) subtitled the *Divine Poem*. All this music was completed over the three months of summer, 1903. He presented the pile of manuscripts to Belaieff in the autumn as a surprise.

One of the most glowing venerations of Scriabin also began in this summer of 1903. Boris Pasternak, winner of the Nobel Prize in 1958 for his novel *Dr. Zhivago*, was thirteen that year. The Pasternaks had an adjoining *dacha* with Scriabin in the country near Maloyaroslavetz, on the Kiev railway line, an hour from Moscow. Pasternak's father, Leonid, was the finest portrait painter of the day—his subjects included Tolstoi, Anton Rubinstein, Rilke, and later Lenin—and we owe him some of the most accurate depictions in pastel of Scriabin's appearance. More successfully than photographs, he captured not merely the hand but the gesture, not only the face but the expression.

Boris heard Scriabin's fresh new music through a filter of summer leaves and sun-drenched trees. In various fragments of autobiography and poems, Pasternak throughout his life documented his memories of Scriabin: "My god and idol . . . I loved him to distraction . . . Not only a composer, but an occasion for perpetual congratulation, a personified festival and triumph of Russian culture . . . He conquered me by the freshness of his mind. I was always on his side [his father would sometimes challenge the unleashed expanse of Scriabin's mind], although I scarcely ever knew what he meant . . . I loved music more than anything and Scriabin more than anyone else . . . ."

Man and youth became friends that summer, despite inequalities of experience. Because of Scriabin, Pasternak decided to become a composer. A later meeting in 1909 veered Boris from music to literature. He became disillusioned by the fact that Scriabin, his god, not only did not have absolute pitch, but failed to admit it honestly to him. Today, in retrospect, connections between Pasternak's writing and Scriabin's music are well pointed out. Christopher Palmer, the English critic, imputes to Scriabin some of Pasternak's exquisite descriptive passages in poems and novels. He finds some of Scriabin's personal traits in the character of Uncle Kolya in *Zhivago*. When Pasternak died in 1960, pianist Sviatoslav Richter paid fitting tribute from one idol to the other: He held vigil by the corpse playing Scriabin's music all night long.

In the summer of 1903, among the many decisions and burst of creativity, Scriabin also determined to live abroad. In Europe, he said, he would find "true freedom . . . new ideas can flourish there . . . our Russian life, particularly in Moscow, where we do not know how to adjust to the present, is little suited to my exercising those disciplines so needed by my work." Europe, he was sure, would accept his quickly evolving, ever more complex style of music, which was simultaneously growing subsidiary to his developing "ideas" or "world conceptions." He would be recognized more fully and widely abroad, and therefore would earn more money and arrive at the independence on which any man's freedom of spirit is based.

He stayed on foreign soil for five years without once returning to Russia. He certainly became more famous living abroad, almost proving that a prophet is without honor in his own country. But in one sense he was wrong in his 1903 thought. His greatest successes and farthest reaching responses first came when he revisited Russia in 1909, and later when he settled in Moscow for good in 1910.

Some Soviet musicologists take pains to say that Scriabin's peregrinations abroad were a "serious mistake." Had

he remained in Russia during those crucial years—1904–9
—he would have been in touch with political events there.
His Socialist tendencies might have flowered and snuffed
the mystical side of his nature. "The first Russian Revolution," Lev Danilevich wrote, "could have beneficially influenced the thought and development of Scriabin as it
did Alexander Blok."

This juggles history by misreading the future. Most Russian intellectuals, particularly the writers and musicians, no
matter how "revolutionary" they were under Tsardom,
were hostile to Bolshevism, including Maxim Gorki who
was personally friendly with Lenin. By 1919 however, some
poets publicly did respond to the Revolution in their own
way. Alexander Blok (originally a mystic like Scriabin) in his
extraordinary poem "The Twelve," unlikely enough likens
twelve Red Guards to apostles led by the invisible Christ
crowned with roses. Valeri Briussov and Andrei Biely also
wrote poems which wedded mysticism and Revolution,
Christ and violence.

True enough, Europe did foster the odor of symbolism
in Scriabin's music and stir the decadence of his Paris
years. Belgium was a stronghold of Theosophy, under the
spell of its founder Helena Blavatsky. She, by fixing a table
with her eyes, could render it unliftable even by muscle-
men. Her pan-religiosity embraced every faith, including
all claims by saints and mystics to supernatural powers.
(When Blavatsky was exposed in 1914 as a "fraud," Scriabin reacted protectively by saying that all truly great people
were subject to that kind of trumped up "ignominy.") But
Theosophy stimulated Scriabin's overall purpose—that of
"making the impossible possible." (We will pursue this
point in Chapter VI.) He also learned about Rudolf
Steiner and Anthroposophy in Switzerland.

According to Soviet reasoning, Europe further Europeanized Scriabin, and his music became less intensively Russian. This, in the perspective of time, as we saw earlier, is not so. And it was certainly not the case with Rachmaninov and Grechaninov who left Russia at the same time and for the same reasons, hoping for greater fortunes abroad than at home, long before the Revolution and again after.

Money was always at the root of Scriabin's physical suffering (in contradistinction to his mental anguish), and it was the motive for his incredible industry over the summer of 1903. The more pieces he turned out, the more cash he would earn. Oddly, the quality of these many, new and varied masterpieces was not affected by their bulk. Among them were the eight Etudes Op. 42, among the best "études of experience" (rather than "études of difficulties," or "picture-études") to be found in piano literature, the caressing, kissing Poem Op. 32. No. 1, and the "Satanic Poem" Op. 36, which was Belaieff's favorite.

Some of the thirty-six pieces are seconds-long miniatures, the brilliant Prelude Op. 37 No. 2, for example, or the half-page Albumleaf (without opus number, and incorrectly attributed to 1905).*

Scriabin's earlier period of laconic gusts of inspiration has been described by writer Arnold Alshvang as Scriabin's "principle of composing short compositions of highest impulse with fullest expanse." Almost as if justifying his past, Scriabin now strove for condensation. "I want the maximum expression with the minimum means," he often said. The microcosm is contained within the macrocosm, and the reverse is also true. All is one. Less is more. If a poem

---

* Albumleaf was written to be published in a collection. The proceeds of the collection were to benefit the widows and orphans of members of the Russian Musical Society Orchestra.

can be a quatrain and a sonnet can speak universal, total truth, why not a fourteen-measure piece or a prelude of four lines, he asked.

One principle obsessed him: "From the greatest delicacy (refinement), via active efficacy (flight) to the greatest grandiosity." And on the basis of this maxim Scriabin vacillated between vast scores and brief fragments of music. Some of his preludes were "shorter than a sparrow's beak, briefer than a bear's tail," as one critic wrote. The phrase caught on. Strangely, several people have recorded that when Scriabin played his miniatures in private, they never sounded so short as they did in concert.

Short and long, the enormous quantity of music in 1903 entranced Belaieff. Never before in nine years of their friendship had he been more satisfied with Scriabin as artist or as workman. He augmented Scriabin's personal stipend to $100 a month, which made the sojourn abroad more realistic. However, with Belaieff's death at the end of the year, the firm's office claimed no knowledge of this personal stipulation. The advisory board (Rimsky, Glazunov and Liadov) together with the board of directors canceled the stipend.

Without the presence of Belaieff and his fortune, the firm was forced to try to become self-supporting. They further retrenched by reducing fees paid for compositions from its huge roster of Russian composers.

In the autumn of 1903, Margarita Morozova, the wealthy widow (and, it was rumored, bearer of Scriabin's child after her husband's death), promised Scriabin $100 a month, thinking of it as a supplement to Belaieff's amount. She came to Switzerland next spring for a holiday together with her children, wet nurse, governess, and a tutor for her son. Scriabin, having left Moscow earlier in January, 1904, rented a villa for her across the lake from him with its own private park and gardens. Scriabin had found for himself, Vera and the children (although he had planned on installing his family far away in Dresden), a very small, two-story house in Vézénaz, a village near Geneva. From the workroom upstairs, where the worn-out upright teetered, you could see the lake and the mountains. Guests sat at the little table in the garden, and listened to the music wafting down from overhead.

When Morozova saw Scriabin's dreadful piano, she ordered a splendid grand from Bern. (There was not a piano for rent in all of Geneva.) The night it arrived, Scriabin was so impatient he unpacked it in the garden. He sat there under the stars of night, playing the Fourth Sonata and its "music of flight into space." After this impulsive concert, the piano was hoisted up to the balcony on the second floor. Scriabin played at parties among friends as was his liking, or to relax after lessons.

By 1903, Scriabin had resolved to make Vera divorce him. This too made leaving Russia and going abroad a necessity. The additional reason for Scriabin's self-exile was Tatyana. They had first met when she was barely fifteen. Now, after many protestations and much vacillation she had agreed to become his mistress, only until Vera agreed to a divorce, she thought. Poor Tatyana. It was not until Scriabin lay on his deathbed, as Sabaneeff tells the story, that the Tsar legalized the relationship and officially entitled their children to the Scriabin name.

Tatyana had three children by Scriabin, two girls and a boy. Julian, the only other Scriabin to show musical talent, composed four little preludes—in a style which begins almost where Scriabin ends—when he was a mere ten. Canadian pianist Anton Kuerti writes of these preludes that "they are so startlingly good, one is left with the choice between suspicion that they were derived from sketches of unpublished works of his father, supplied by his mother, or that the twentieth-century was tragically robbed of one of its greatest musical talents." But we have the testament of Julian's originality from his professor of composition at the Kiev Conservatory, Reinhold Glière. In 1919 Julian drowned in the Dnieper River just as he turned eleven years of age.

Scriabin's marriage to Tatyana began and ended with his having affairs with other women. To supplement his income while he was teaching at the Moscow Conservatory, Scriabin taught an additional day a week at the Catherine Institute for Girls. In 1903, he seduced one of the fifteen-year-old students, and gossip alone would have forced him out of Moscow. Scriabin scandals were bruited news of the day, and when we read memoirs and reminiscences by his contemporaries, it is hard to winnow lurid speculation from fact. The likelihood of truth in this instance, however, is always present.

More definite and less of a rumor was Scriabin's wish to leave Tatyana shortly before his death in 1915. After returning from a series of London triumphs, Scriabin began a love affair with a married woman. They agreed to abandon their respective homes and "make life together," according to Kashperov who knew the woman and her husband, both of whom outlived Scriabin. Still, Tatyana and Scriabin, despite the turmoil and a hardship that poverty imposed abroad in 1904, spent happy days and nights together. He loved her, and under her unflinching belief in him, composed spectacularly daring music of meta- and mega-harmonies. However, according to some of their friends, Tatyana basked in the reflection of Scriabin's light and fame and abused her privilege as wife of the great composer. She spun a web of constantly tightening possessiveness around him.

In Switzerland, where he first settled ("country of Rousseau," he thought, forgetting it was also Calvin's homeland), Scriabin's closest friend was a common fisherman, Otto Hauenstein. Otto was a big, burly man of no education, but he was someone who truly loved Scriabin. He called him "Alexandre," and there were not many people who used first names with Scriabin. (As the visions inside Scriabin's head had sharpened, he eschewed personal intimacy.) Otto put his arm around Scriabin in public, which shocked Russians who saw them. He and his fishermen cronies were Socialist firebrands, who surrounded Scriabin's table at the local tavern, drinking and agreeing that "Money must be abolished . . . Poverty must vanish . . . Everyone should do only what he wants . . . ." They also "believed" in Scriabin, but not because of his music. Otto's only recorded comment after a Scriabin concert was, "What a lot of noise Alexandre makes." They regarded him as a prophet. They had memorized lines from *Acts* of the Bible which substantiated their religious Communism: "And all that believed were together, and had all things in common; and sold their possessions and goods and parted them to all men as every man needs."

Scriabin liked to stand on a chair in the tavern and expound and expatiate on his dreams and schemes. Once he tried to imitate Christ—so certain he was of his miraculous powers—by walking on the waters of Lake Geneva. Failing, he settled for preaching to the fishermen from a boat.

This alarmed Vera, as much as did his demands for a divorce. She busily went about asking friends whether they thought Scriabin was really spiritual, was actually capable of founding a new cult, and recommended that he submit himself to a religious inquest adjudicated by priests and qualified clergy. Those who came within Scriabin's orbit were impressed. Even a prominent critic as sound as Yuri Engel (he later was Boris Pasternak's composition teacher) who visited Scriabin during this period of open messianism, felt that whatever the quirks, the music was worth the candle.

It also was at this time that Scriabin gave up wearing hats. Someone had said hats were bad for the hair. Since it was considered outrageous and ungentlemanly for a man to appear bareheaded in public, he always pinned a hat to his coat to show that he actually owned one. Throughout Europe, street urchins would run after him, chanting and taunting: "Mister without a hat."

Scriabin made many friends in Europe. In the beginning they were mostly drinking companions, but some were artists of quondam importance. Unfortunately, their names have lost significance with the passage of time. Many tended in their thinking toward the most blatantly mystical and Theosophical contentions.

One of the major friendships in Scriabin's life, and one dialectically opposed to his other relationships, was with Georgi Plekhanov. On the Italian Riviera late in 1905, when the two men met and drew close, Plekhanov was fifty-one years old. He was a confirmed Marxist, a strict Socialist, and one of the most outstanding revolutionists in history. He even was called "Architect of the Russian Revolution." As an exile, and later, as leader of the Mensheviki, he, by the thinnest of margins, was to be defeated by the less cultivated leader of the Bolsheviki, V. I. Lenin.

Plekhanov loved Scriabin. "What a sympathetic and talented man," he said, "but an incorrigible mystic." He found Scriabin's mental processes "brilliant," full of "native intellect," although the skimpy Cadet Corps tuition had left gaps in his education.

Whether he agreed or not, the working of Scriabin's mind enchanted Plekhanov. They argued every day they were together, and the friendship continued in Switzerland the following year. Instead of becoming estranged, their intimacy deepened. Plekhanov on one hand represented dogmatic rationality. Scriabin on the other possessed a fuzzy, muddled mysticism, poisonous to revolutionaries. Plekhanov influenced Scriabin enormously. As a result, he liked to say at that time that his music "chimes in with and presupposes the coming Revolution." He toyed with the idea of using a slogan to caption the *Poem of Ecstasy,* "Arise, ye wretched of the earth."

When the 1905 Revolution erupted, Scriabin, like all Russians living abroad, had been deeply affected. "We take the news from Russia very much to heart, and while we read all that is happening we experience many a sad moment," he wrote. Another time he said "The *political* revolution in Russia in its present phase and the upheaval I want are different. Of course, this revolution like every disruption brings the beginning of my desired moment closer. I am wrong to say 'upheaval.' I don't want to *bring about anything* except the endless soaring of creative activity which my art will bring." He saw both as the approach of his *prazdnik* or "festival." However, as Soviet musicologist Victor Delson observes, "Scriabin was far from understanding political events. He approached them more as an artist. . . ."

Scriabin came under suspicion after the 1918 Revolution. Plekhanov, with his unimpeachable background from having suffered under the Tsar and engineering his downfall, defended him. Never once wavering from his certitude as to Scriabin's genius, he explained, "When an era finds itself expressed in the creative work of a great artist, this earns eternal significance. The times lose all importance."

Scriabin was a revolutionary in music, and he was sympathetic to Socialist ideals. He despised high society, at least until the very last years or so of his life. Even when he was in his "socializing" period and in love with the beautiful and elegant Natalya (her parents would not let him marry her, because they thought he was neither rich nor famous nor well-born enough for her—but he was), he spoke of his "social servitude," of his "slavery," meaning not that he had to sit below the salt at table as Mozart did, but that he had to see and be seen at salons in order to become known.

Already in 1905 in Paris, pushing through a performance of the *Divine Poem*, and drumming up a ticket-buying audience for his recitals, he played teatime recitals and performed in soirées in the mansions of Parisian and expatriate Russian princes and princesses, all as part of an "artist's obligation." He spoke of their "stupidest of idle chatter," although at one of these gatherings he met pianist Ossip Gabrilowitch and conductor Felix Weingartner doing the same thing to advance their own careers. "What an empty and foolish life I lead . . . playing before imbeciles drives me mad," he wrote Vera.

In 1906, on the boat going to America he wrote Tatyana, "Never in my life have I been in such close proximity to the 'privileged' class of so many well-fed idiots." After landing in America, he was irritated by "idiotic questions," and Safonov cautioned him not to "ruffle American bourgeois sense of well-being." Like any composer, Scriabin needed all the "financial well-wishers" he could find, irrespective of Revolution or Socialism.

In May, 1905, Morozova gave Scriabin the backing to

subsidize a performance of the *Divine Poem* in Paris. Artur Nikisch, who would conduct anything or teach anyone for money, received $750. Another $750 was set aside to cover other expenses for the concert. "This will be the first public proclamation of my doctrine," Scriabin wrote Morozova. Paris newspapers billed the piece as "a grandiose creation which transports the listener fantastically into another world and bases itself on a philosophical content."

The performance was called a "manifestation," and everyone expected something extraordinary to happen. Vera came unannounced from Vézénaz to Paris for the première. Scriabin and Tatyana stayed in rooms at a hotel across town. The audience applauded. The concert was a respectable success. Afterward, Scriabin challenged his manager to a duel, because he had not returned an adequate percentage of the proceeds.

Undaunted by the visible fact that nothing beyond recognition resulted from the *Divine Poem*, he immediately began work on the *Poem of Ecstasy*. His ideas were steadily crystallizing, and he codified them. He explained endlessly to Morozova, in a souvenir from Dr. Erb, that by analyzing oneself psychologically, by studying oneself, man can explain everything, including the whole cosmos.

Thinking intuitively and expressing himself by analogy, he tried to convert everyone—including priests. He lectured that the Creator appears in the world as one man whose superindividualistic "I" opens up by means of his own introspection. There is no higher will, no moral norm over this superindividualistic "I." "I am God." All is one, by the very nature of itself, but it spreads itself out as "I" and "Thou," spirit and matter, male and female, only to return to the one Unity.

Morozova at first thought Scriabin was dreaming or imagining when he said that he himself, his "I," stood at the center of world evolution, that he would bring about the transformation of the world by means of art, and return it to original Oneness. When she realized he was concretely in earnest, "a very complicated struggle began in my soul . . . but I didn't want to hurt his feelings . . . it was so interesting to hear." As Sabaneeff would say, "Even if you didn't *believe* him, at least you *wanted* to."

Scriabin wrote Tatyana, "I bow before the great sensitivity you tender toward HE who dwells within me. You now believe in Him. HE is great, though I am at times poor, little, weak and weary. But you forgive me all this because HE lives in me. I am not yet HE, but soon I will become HE! Patience, and believe, believe. HE will identify Himself within me."

But he did not yield entirely to his HE. As he said to Schloezer, "I swear to you that if I was certain that there was someone else greater than I who could create a greater joy on earth than I can, then I would exit immediately and cede my place to him. Naturally, I would stop living." And Scriabin often referred to himself in the third person the way children or schizophrenics do. "A composer whom you know . . ." he would say, or "a certain Scriabine . . ." he would write while directly referring to himself to an intimate friend.

Critic Arnold Alshvang heard Scriabin say on one occasion, "I don't know anything I can't express at the piano, and from these different expressions I can build an entire system as an inner entirety or whole. And it seems to me that musical expression is much more pointedly logical in its descriptive powers than any abstract concepts."

Heady, solipsistic stuff, all this. Soviet musicologist Olga Sedelnikova, writing a review of Scriabin's *Letters* in *Musical Life*, Issue No. 1, 1972, warns her reader, while such statements smack of "self-love," they were made only to his closest intimates, "and can be explained by Scriabin's belief in the high role of the artist and only partly in himself. . . ."

In 1906 Scriabin broke with the Belaieff firm. For a time —precisely when he was composing his best music to date— he languished without any publisher. An Austrian house suggested that Scriabin write waltzes at $25 each. He refused.

The split arrived without overt acrimony, but with a sufficiency of behind-the-back jokes. Scriabin was congenitally quick to take offense at any real or imagined (sometimes quite invented) slight. Now, his vanity, always mortgaged to sensitivity, was fiercely aggravated by his desperate poverty from maintaining two households—Vera and Tatyana. Unborne out as he had been about Europe's superiority over Russia in comprehending his music, he was right about the price tag he set on his pieces. These included the superlative, nearly intangible "Fragility" Op. 51 No. 1 and "Dance of Languor" No. 4 "Poem of Languor" Op. 52 No. 3, "Ironies" Op. 56 No. 2, as well as "Danced Caress" and "Desire" Op. 57. These last two were originally designed to be a pair of orchestral miniatures, but because of his haste to earn money he left them as sketches in piano form. Scriabin wanted $150 to $200 for each piece. The Belaieff firm paid him $50, without explaining the change in their pay scale.

Liadov made a notation in 1906 on the grab bag set of Four Pieces Op. 51, "Since Scriabin won't accept five kopecks per prelude, which is all such short pieces are worth, we might as well pay him four hundred rubles," a remarkable remark coming from a miniaturist himself. The irrevocable rupture came in 1908, and Liadov might have done well to look at those pieces more carefully.

Invited by his Conservatory friend Modest Altschuler, Scriabin made a short concert tour in America at the end of 1906 and early 1907. He played his Concerto with Safonov at Carnegie Hall, substituted for Gabrilowitch in Detroit, and recitaled with moderate success in New York, Cincinnati and Chicago. He came to America, a country which to his surprise pleased him, partly for money (which was not much), and partly to escape for a while from Tatyana. Her rule over him had grown oppressive. He did everything in his power to dissuade her from joining him. Since his second child had recently arrived and was still nursing, he threatened that if she came the infant would starve. He told her how horrible the ocean was in winter. He terrified her with stories of Maxim Gorki, the writer, who had been expelled from America the year before on a morals charge because he had brought along his mistress. But Tatyana, undeterred, came anyway.

The Scriabins were not expelled, but Safonov did answer truthfully, when a reporter asked him, that the real Mme. Scriabina was in Moscow and not the lady at present in America. Scriabin never quite forgave Safonov—it precipitated his early departure from America—because whatever his tribulations with Tatyana, he did love her, loved her faith in him, and needed her as an aid and inspiration to composition. He also worked unceasingly to legitimize their common-law relationship. The story of Scriabin's life, too, is spattered with broken friendships, because one person or another failed, however politely, to receive Tatyana in Moscow society as his wife.

One evening in later years, while talking with painter Nikolai Ulyanov, whose portraits of Stanislavsky and Chekhov are famous, Scriabin recalled his four-month visit to America. He described how his manager arranged for him to meet with reporters and interviewers. "I didn't speak English, but this wasn't necessary. My impresario spoke for me. He installed me without asking in the most expensive [$10.00 a day] hotel with a whole suite, not just a room. It has to be this way, he said. I had lost my trunks, and felt homeless when I was left in the suite he chose for me. Next morning he brought me all the newspapers with my history, picture, and even quotes from me which I never said. If anyone wanted me because of my music, I don't know. But everywhere I went I met with triumph. America loves noise and publicity . . . After such 'success,' there was only one thing left—to return from that country spangled with dollars. But things turned out otherwise."

Scriabin, after his initial flurry, was dropped in America. He left the country with only a handful of dollars, and a number of unpaid bills for which he was dunned by mail. (The demands are on file at the Scriabin Museum.) After arriving in Paris, he had barely 30 francs. He more formally described his American experience for the *Russian Musical Gazette:* "I was very favorably impressed by America, and I think that Europeans judge America most immaturely and onesidedly. Americans are far from insensitive and un-talented in art, as is generally thought."

The letters which Scriabin wrote Tatyana before she came to America to join him, and to Altschuler (he signed these "Pussy") after Scriabin had returned to Paris, are astonishing. The reader cannot tell, sometimes, whether the writer is male or female, so kittenish, coy and affection-ate are they in tone and effusiveness. When Scriabin felt his elevation of feeling, a kind of psychic euphoria—"Again I am swept by an enormous wave of creativity. I choke for breath, but oh what bliss! I am composing di-vinely . . ."—he reaches near incoherence. He associated his ecstatic inner states with "uplift" or "upsurge," *podyom*, which others think of more commonly as inspiration. His letters to Tatyana reveal a helplessly dependent man ("I need you, oh how I need you") who resents his very dependence.

His increasing concertizing away from home, it would seem, was not so much for money or in response to demand, as it was to free himself from Tatyana and for domestic respite. Appearing before the public as a performer was good propaganda for the Scriabin's cause, but it vastly disrupted his schedule of composing. These concerts also pricked the thesis of "I-am-God" ballooning in his mind. Morozova remembered one night after a concert when he said to her, "Look, I prepare myself for a world role, and yet coming out on stage before an audience is always a real ordeal!"

In the spring of 1907, shortly after Scriabin's return from America, the "Five Historical Concerts of Russian Music from Glinka to Scriabin" took place in Paris, at the Grand Opera. Rachmaninov, also being played as a composer during the series, should have been listed at the terminal point since he was younger by a year, but Scriabin's name was better known. These concerts were organized by Sergei Diaghilev, together with Alexander Taneyev (no relation to the composer), a wealthy statesman. They were in part propaganda for Russia, as well as a financial undertaking by Diaghilev who, for all his innovative genius, rarely ignored the public as a source of profit.

From 16 to 30 May (New Style), 1907, Paris was jammed with Russian musicians. All of Moscow and St. Petersburg, artists and patrons, were there. They went en masse one night to a performance of Debussy's *Pelléas et Mélisande*. The Russians usually met at the Café de la

Paix to talk away the night among themselves. It was one night at Scriabin's "tiny, charming apartment with soft furniture newly covered with pale yellow silk," on a quiet residential street, 24 rue de la Tour, that Rimsky and Scriabin met for the last time.

Scriabin's relationship with Rimsky (or "Korsakov," as he called him) has often been misinterpreted. In his book *My Musical Life*, Rimsky described his first meeting with Scriabin at one of Belaieff's musical Fridays, and wrote that he was "somewhat warped, affected and self-opinionated . . . Of Scriabin I shall speak later on." Rimsky died before that "later on" arrived and he could finish his memoirs. Even at their first meeting, Rimsky recognized that Scriabin was "a star of first magnitude," and said so. Had he lived, he almost certainly would have written more sympathetically.

As it is, we must depend on their correspondence and the reminiscences of their contemporaries for a fuller picture of Rimsky's and Scriabin's acquaintance. The two men met socially, and as occasions made possible they worked together professionally. Rimsky was the decisive vote in the Belaieff Publishing House as to what was or was not published. Certainly, Scriabin's music was always printed, although in one instance, Rimsky selected the present, well-known version of Scriabin's masterpiece, the Etude in D♯ Minor Op. 8 No. 12, instead of its alternate version.

Scriabin had sent both manuscripts to Belaieff saying that he simply could not make up his mind between the two. The alternate version is more interesting, more erratic, more Scriabinic (hence Rimsky's choice for the other). The second theme is in a major key. There is extra drama throughout, and a more exciting climax at the end. Unfortunately, too, the pianissimo (*pp*) ending which Scriabin marked in both versions is omitted in the Belaieff edition, doubtless another Rimsky suggestion based on his more conventional concept of how a "warhorse" should end in a blaze of volume as well as glory.

Rimsky's wife, Nadezhda Purgold, like all wives in Scriabin's life, adored Scriabin. Her few pages of reminiscence written in 1917, two years after Scriabin's death and a year before her own, indicate her feeling. She records that when Scriabin played the *Poem of Ecstasy* for Rimsky in Paris at this last, 1907, meeting, he found it "delightful in various themes and passages," although overall he regretted a certain "sameness," and the harmonies seemed "too spicy . . . with unmitigated tension."

Morozova has also left her memory of that same evening. Instead of the Café de la Paix, the Russians met at 24 rue de la Tour after one of the Historical Concerts. Rimsky had conducted some of his own music. Nikisch had conducted Scriabin's Second Symphony. Hofmann had played Scriabin's Concerto, and the Third Sonata. Chaliapin had sung. At the Scriabins were Rimsky and his wife, Rachmaninov, Glazunov, Hofmann with his new American wife, and Morozova.

Everyone was curious about the *Poem of Ecstasy*, which had been scheduled, and even the first page of the manuscript (in Scriabin's excessively neat orthography) had appeared in facsimile on the cover of the souvenir program. Although the music was written, the scoring was still incomplete. Scriabin played it on the rented piano in the parlor. Afterward, he sat with Rimsky and "reluctantly, almost as if it was his duty to explain," expounded its philosophic basis and his ideas of world view and world construction. Morozova heard Scriabin say, "You will live with all sensations, with harmonies of sounds, harmonies of colors, harmonies of perfume!" Rimsky winced. "That I don't understand," he said, "I don't understand music of scents," although both composers had the gift or ability of synesthesia or photism and were able, from birth, to see colors while hearing tones. Morozova concluded her description of the meetings saying that the men were not "enemies," only "worlds apart" in understanding and as people. In June, 1908, while Scriabin was giving a piano lesson to Canadian pianist Alfred Laliberté, he learned by telegram of Rimsky's death. He left the room and wept for half an hour.

May of 1907 led to a tense incident between Scriabin and Diaghilev. Diaghilev had been late in sending complimentary tickets to one of the Historical Concerts. At intermission, Scriabin lashed out at him.

"I was almost late . . ."

"Be glad I sent the tickets at all."

"Without artists like me, who would want to know you," Scriabin shouted at Diaghilev. And friends of the warped, posing and self-opinionated Diaghilev were flabbergasted when he dropped the matter, mumbling, "I meant no harm . . ." If this dispute sound simple, it was not. It was the first time that Scriabin had ever lost his temper so publicly, and the first time Diaghilev ever apologized to anyone.

Diaghilev was very much a man to hold grudges. Nevertheless, in 1910 he wanted to make a ballet of Scriabin's Fifth Symphony, *Prometheus: the Poem of Fire* Op. 60. Scriabin excused himself, perhaps because he did hold grudges, or possibly because he had always been curiously embarrassed by ballet. The exposed legs and thighs of ballerinas, or ballerins, unnerved him. His attitude is all the more peculiar, as one looks back, considering that doing pirouettes was as close as he ever came to athletic activity. There was even a period in his twenties, "socializing," when he went around walking like a ballerina with splayed feet and pointing his toes outward as he sat. Diaghilev later dissuaded George Balanchine from any further Scriabiniana ballets. In Balanchine's St. Petersburg years, he had danced and choreographed Scriabin's music. His music was used widely by dancers in Russia then, much as it is abroad today. (Most notably and recently, in John Cranko's *Poem of Ecstasy*, created for the Stuttgart Ballet in Germany and which followed Rudolf Nureyev's disastrous choreography to the same music; Stephen Simmons' choreography to the Concerto for the San Francisco Ballet; and Joe Layton's *Double Exposure* for the Joffrey Ballet in New York. This last work has a homosexual episode danced to Scriabin's piano vignette titled "Strangeness" Op. 63 No. 2, in an echo of the 1939 ballet to all-Scriabin music, *Les Forces Errantes*, scripted by Cornelius Conyn and performed in Brussels and Paris.)

In 1908, another celebrated name entered Scriabin's life, Serge Koussevitzky, better known to us as the conductor of the Boston Symphony Orchestra from 1924 until 1949. "I would not have perished without him," Scriabin once cried after he had angrily broken off their relationship, "but he surely would have perished without *me!*"

Koussevitzky, who built his early career on Scriabin's glistening reputation, was a much disliked man in musical Russia. He was Jewish, although a converted Christian, and he was considered the worst type of parvenu bourgeois. He had married Natalya Ushakova, who was plain, but one of the richest heiresses in all Russia. His first wife had been a poor ballerina at the Bolshoi, and he himself was a bass viol player in that orchestra at a salary of $50 a month.

Among the many grandiose projects inspired and made possible by his new wife's new money, in 1908 Koussevitzky established the S. and N. Koussevitzky "Russian

Music Edition," a rival of Belaieff's publishing firm. Scriabin was the first composer to be approached. This was originally the idea of Natalya—negotiated by the ever devoted Monighetti sisters—and a further indication of that pattern in Scriabin's life of wives. Unfortunately, the contract was never put in writing. It was a "gentleman's agreement" based on their respective words of honor.

Scriabin was living in Switzerland, in a little village outside of Lausanne on the lake. The Koussevitzkys paid a formal call. It was the first time Scriabin had ever ridden in an automobile, and a liveried chauffeur-driven one at that. His vast projected composition, the "Mysterium," had already been mentioned in the newspapers, and the idea of synthesizing all the arts of sound, sight, color, lights, touch and scents, appealed to Koussevitzky and his wife. Koussevitzky asked how long it would take to complete. "Five years," Scriabin, unrealistic as usual, answered. Koussevitzky proposed paying Scriabin $2,500 (five thousand rubles) a year beginning instantly, against which Koussevitzky would also publish all Scriabin music written during that time.

The meeting went splendidly. The Koussevitzkys asked the Scriabins to come and visit them in fashionable Biarritz and escape the summer heat. They went. Koussevitzky paid the sculptor Seraphin Soudbinin to do a bust of Scriabin. Koussevitzky also added Soudbinin to his roster of artists to design covers for Scriabin compositions to come.

Scriabin thought that his supra-musical magnawork, "Mysterium," would be so potent in effect that the world would be destroyed in its final "festival," not just changed as by "Revolution." Koussevitzky was gullible, although he knew that whatever its ultimate intent, Scriabin's music was commercially viable, attracting a larger and larger public. He said, privately, that the actual effect of the performance of the "Mysterium" would probably be no more than "We will all go out and have a fine dinner afterward. . . ."

IV   Russian Return

The arrangement with Koussevitzky in 1908 saved Scriabin financially. He had a publisher again and a regular income. The *Poem of Ecstasy* was finished, and his son Julian arrived simultaneously with the celebrations. In Koussevitzky, Scriabin also had an ardent propagandist, although many Russians at that time scorned Koussevitzky as "the upstart conductor" (*dirizhorvyskochka*).

Koussevitzky's first expenditure was for private lessons with Nikisch. Whatever his lacks as an orchestral conductor—and Rachmaninov carried over into America Russian sneering at Koussevitzky—his inherent affinity for Scriabin was phenomenal. He conducted Scriabin magnificently. Even Sabaneeff the scandalmonger admitted that "Koussevitzky's innate conductor's temperament and the delicacy of his orchestral feeling were extraordinarily suited to the performance of Scriabin's music. His closeness to the composer gave him easy access to the most secret of Scriabin's thoughts, his ideas and worlds of mood."

Scriabin was invited to return to Russia for a series of concerts and programs devoted to his music. The trip was

74

not taken without trepidation, as indicated by a letter of mid-December, 1908, to Alfred Laliberté. "I am very sorry to have caused you upset. Excuse me. I am indeed wicked. But if I have not written in so long, it is because we have had many worries in connection with our trip to Russia, annoying and absorbing matters. Then there has been my work and a thousand other things. . . ."

The Koussevitzkys offered hospitality, which the Scriabins quickly accepted, since the reception of Tatyana as "wife" was a delicate matter. (It was only in late 1905 when their first child was born that Scriabin himself began addressing his mail to her as Mme. Scriabina, instead of Mlle. de Schloezer.) Half of Scriabin's old friends, while they invited him, did not extend their invitations to Mlle. de Schloezer. On one occasion he was sent a single ticket to a concert. Moreover, by staying with the Koussevitzkys, another group of Scriabin's friends would not meet him there, despite the luxury of the princely house furnished lavishly and liberally supplied with butlers, footmen, maids for the chambers and parlors. Koussevitzky, like Tatyana, was not socially acceptable to snobs.

The Scriabins arrived in Moscow at the end of January, 1909. Two of Koussevitzky's sixteen servants met them at the train. Scriabin's first concert was scheduled for 21 February. The Russian-born conductor, Englishman Emil Cooper who had studied the *Poem of Ecstasy* with Scriabin the summer before in Brussels, performed both the Third and Fourth Symphonies. (The rehearsals for *Ecstasy* had turned from the usual two or three into an unprecedented and exorbitant six.) At the same concert Scriabin appeared in person playing the Fifth Sonata, and for encores a string of études, preludes, now standbys in the piano repertoire, and the left-hand pieces.

Boris Schloezer wrote the program notes—following the

pattern Koussevitzky had introduced in Russia—and they
were criticized for being "high-flown and cloudy," that is,
obscurantist and mystical. The concert went off splendidly.
The open, general rehearsal had been thronged with a mix-
ture of the "curious and the learned." The audience at the
actual concert included many faces new to the regular sub-
scribers for the Russian Musical Society's concert series.
The reviews, generally, depicted Scriabin as "a star of first
magnitude." However, when Scriabin asked his old teacher
Taneyev backstage how he had liked the program, Taneyev
barked, "I feel as if I have been beaten with sticks." But
Scriabin's success was repeated in St. Petersburg.

Morozova introduced Scriabin to Andrei Biely. Biely was
already recognized as a master symbolist poet in 1909. He
wrote "symphonies in words," as well as a novel, *St. Petersburg*, about the 1905 Revolution. When published in 1913,
the book galvanized Russia's intellectual circles as "Art of
the City."

Morozova expected the men to become friends. Scriabin
always talked of "the transforming role of art in the
world," and her friend Biely spoke of "premonitions of the
new life." Scriabin's titles for pieces of music were borrow-
ing from the symbolists, she thought, "Winged Poem,"
"Ironies," "Nuances," and the like, and he was shifting
from the familiar Italian markings such as *Allegro* and
Lento into ambiguous directions like "mysterious breath,"
"caressing wave," etc. Scriabin spoke of constructing systemic harmonies, and Biely was writing poetry from alge-
braic formulae, anatomical tables and diagrams.

However, to Morozova's social consternation, Scriabin
and Biely exchanged "not a word with any meaning to it,"
and neither "guessed" the other's significance. Two van-
ities had met and parted without divining the sphere of the
larger world each represented.

In March 1909, the Scriabins, refreshed by the tentative return to Moscow—a trial dipping of toes into the waters of gossip—decided to make their home back in Russia. They returned to Brussels only to tie up loose ends of living arrangements, to prepare the children for the venture, and to allow Scriabin to finish *Prometheus*. He had written it in full outline, but would not finish the orchestration until mid-1910.

For the remainder of 1909, Scriabin's life was simple. He saw Tatyana's relatives (she was half Belgian), walked for an hour or two every day, and watched over the children, to whom the parents spoke entirely in French. (This was the custom among upper class Russians—even Aunt Lyubov had been sent to the French lycée in Moscow.) He went to the theater and opera. Strauss's *Salomé* fared better than Wagner. He liked the Wilde libretto. As for Wagner, he wrote, "Heard *Walküre* . . . Impression exactly what I felt about *Siegfried*. Two or three enchanting moments. All the rest frightfully dull." He read voraciously —*Life of Buddha*, *Religion in India*, *Light of Asia*, and Blavatsky.

In January 1910, the entire Scriabin family with Tatyana's mother who served as baby-sitter, housekeeper and French governess, arrived back in Moscow to take up permanent residence. Vera welcomed the couple with one of her all-Scriabin recitals, and she and Safonov (to whom Scriabin no longer spoke) performed the Concerto together. Scriabin was "humiliated," he said, meaning "infuriated."

Koussevitzky played *Ecstasy* with his newly hired, personal orchestra, and dangled garlands of Christmas lights from the proscenium. Scriabin was pleased, although he muttered to a friend, "Frightfully vulgar . . . but never mind." After the performance, while the applause was still

thundering, Koussevitzky said (not within Scriabin's hearing), "This is the greatest composition in all music. But
only the devil knows what it is!"

In the late spring of 1910, Koussevitzky effected one of
his gaudiest schemes. He hired his old alma mater orchestra
from the Bolshoi, and with Scriabin as piano soloist and
violinist Alexander Mogilevsky (to whom violinists today
owe many transcriptions of Scriabin music), went by
steamship all the way down the thousand miles of the
Volga River from Tver to Astrakhan. They stopped at
each of the eleven major cities on the river and gave two
concerts in each—one of Russian music, the other of Western staples in the musical diet.

The significance of this trip was epochal, and its ramifi-
cations were far-reaching. It was the first time that the
provinces ever were exposed to such a body of serious music
performed by first rank artists. While the untutored audiences may have learned from the Western program, in
general they preferred the Russian one. Scriabin played his
gentle Concerto ten times (how he hated going over his
early compositions!), and left the troupe early to return to
Moscow.

In 1910 as in 1902, Scriabin composed nothing aside
from the fragmentary Poem and Prelude Op. 59, and probably the Albumleaf Op. 58, really a nocturne, as was so
much of Scriabin's music. The Albumleaf is a splinter
piece of *Prometheus*, germane to the past but seminal of
the ripe, overripe and rich music to come. These two pages
—concentrated as a sonnet—are basic study requisite for
anyone approaching the last arcana of Scriabin's music.
(See Chapter VIII page 148). The piece was published
by Koussevitzky in 1911 in a collection, *New Music*. Other
composers represented were Taneyev with a Prelude and
Fugue, Rachmaninov with a Polka, and so forth.

All of 1910 Scriabin was busy with "mechanicals," copy-
ing the score of *Prometheus*. Springtime, when the sap of
inspiration rose highest (as he himself said, identifying
with nature), was dissipated by the Volga tour. The core of
the summer, the time he always worked most prolifically,
was spent in thought.

1910 too was a year for renewing old acquaintances,
mending breaches, making new friends, and "socializing"
to celebrate his triumphal return home. He began going to
the theater regularly, and involving himself seriously in the
"representational arts." Scriabin had long turned his back
on classical ballet. He still disposed of it now as "acrobatics
. . . restricted by traditions." But his new music centering
around the grandiose "Mysterium" demanded the unification of music and dance, as well as the other arts. He had
begun to think of melodies beginning in sound "ending in
gesticulation." Isadora Duncan appeared in Russia with
her "free dance," and despite Scriabin deploring the "old-
fashioned music" she danced to and the embarrassment
her bare feet and exposed contours caused him, he acknowledged her new kind of liberated dance as useful to his
work, a choreography of symbolic gestures.

Victor Delson writes that dance to Scriabin was "not
choreography" so much as it was a visible "plastic magic of
rhythms." As naturally as colors sprang from tones, to him,
movement was an incarnation of rhythmic pulsation for
the eye. Scriabin wanted what he called "pantomime," but
this was to be a stage action without any particular story
or "theatricality" in the accepted sense. He said that the
Orient, particularly India, preserved in its dance language
those philosophical underpinnings which both contained
and communicated a primordial, spiritual potency. Of
course, he never saw Indian dance. When Hanako, a Japa-
nese dancer, appeared in Moscow riding on a reputation

which distinguished her as having been Rodin's mistress, Scriabin found her "unoriental." He was disgruntled that she did not conform to his preconceptions of "spiritual Asia," a reckoning that has beleaguered many persons experiencing Asia both then and since.

Throughout 1910 and into the season of 1911, Scriabin closely watched and studied the freshets of experiments which were flooding Moscow's highly active theater world. Inconsistently he scoffed at Vsevolod Meyerhold for dispensing with footlights, although Scriabin himself was planning ways of removing the separations between "active participants and passive spectators" for his forthcoming "stage work." He thought Meyerhold's innovations "ludicrous" and "a trick." He preferred Yevgeni Vakhtangov of the Free Theater and, above all, Alexander Tairov of the Kamerny Theater (now the Maly).

Scriabin avoided Konstantin Stanislavsky and the atmosphere of the Moscow Art Theater, which he found stuffy, although this was Stanislavsky's short-lived "symbolist period." He personally disliked Nemirovich-Danchenko, the theater's co-founder, and perhaps, by extension, this led him to dislike Meyerhold who had been Danchenko's pupil. However, when the Moscow Art Theater imported the Irish director Gordon Craig to stage *Hamlet*, Scriabin went and was captivated. Craig in this production fused "music, architecture and painting" with theater. Scriabin was particularly fascinated with the backdrop screens which "shimmered in gold." This was complete originality, he said.

Scriabin asked Yurgis Baltrushaitis, a mutual friend, to introduce Craig to him. Baltrushaitis was an extraordinarily distinguished man and a convinced Scriabinist. He was foremost a symbolist poet, both in his native Lithuanian and Russian languages, and with his considerable means

had founded the "Scorpion," a symbolists' publishing firm.
He was literary director for Tairov's Kamerny Theater, and
moved in theatrical circles as well as orbited like a satellite
around Scriabin. Through Scriabin he had hired the very
young Boris Pasternak to tutor his son privately. After the
Revolution, Baltrushaitis's peasant origins stood him in
stead, stamped his credentials, and led to his appointment
as the first Soviet Russian ambassador to Lithuania.

The Scriabin-Craig meetings went well, although Baltrushaitis's intermediary interpreting in English faltered.
Craig spoke no French or Russian, the only languages he
might have had in common with Scriabin. The subjects of
their conversations were difficult—the intricacies of combining all the arts as one. Scriabin also became friendly
with the star of *Hamlet*, Vassili Kachalov, the brilliant
actor who excelled in "intellectual" roles, and who had
made his first sensational impact creating the role of Gaev
in *The Cherry Orchard*.

Scriabin went to every opening of the Kamerny, and
many times saw *Sakuntala*, the Sanskrit play translated by
his friend, poet Vyacheslav Balmont. He approved of its
"lack of theatrical naturalism," particularly Tairov's rhythmic processions and "pantomime" episodes coming in the
middle of the dialogue exchanges. Here he did not seem to
mind the half-naked bodies Tairov used ubiquitously in
order to capture the effect of tropical heat.

As usual, it was the wife who responded profoundly to
Scriabin. Tairov's wife was the celebrated actress Alisa
Koonen, who has left us her memoirs of that year 1910.
The Tairovs dined at the Scriabin apartment and afterward
Scriabin played *Prometheus* for them on the marvelous
Bechstein piano, acquired with the money he was now
earning from his concert fees. Without preparation, Scria-
bin suddenly asked Koonen if she would not like to turn

some of his music into "pantomime." He told her that he wanted to "see" his music "expressed in symbolic gestures." Next day she came, and Scriabin greeted her at the door, saying, "Today you are not a guest. Today we work."

She put on her smock and changed into sandals, and Scriabin played. Saying that these "study periods" were extremely important in the development of her art, Koonen goes on to describe how at first she "interpreted the mood" of this étude or that prelude. Then she began to understand how the music revealed its own shape. Sometimes "an entire subject line" emerged. And together, Koonen and Scriabin created two little *novellas* (using the word in Goethe's definition as "a very short story"), or gesture pieces of interpretive movement with a thread of theme to them. Both artists were pleased by these final results.

During the lesson-experiments, Scriabin drew the blinds of the apartment, and played the piano while simultaneously operating a little circle of table-high colored lights. This was the original *tastiera per luce*, keyboard of light, built for *Prometheus* by Alexander Mozer, a close friend, photographer, and professor of electromechanics at the Moscow School for Higher Technical Training. (Koussevitzky had refused to let Mozer accompany the Volga tour and record its events; instead, he hired Robert Sterl, the German painter, to sketch it.) The apartment was suffused with shifting, different colored lights.

As Scriabin turned more and more attention to the theater and to his poet friends, musicians paid him increasing honor. Pablo Casals, the cellist, visited Russia in 1910 and made a formal call to hear Scriabin's latest music. They talked mostly about Moorish music and Spanish folklore. Scriabin showed special interest in the "daring" of the gypsy harmonies and musical scales. Already he was experimenting in some of those alternating half-tone whole-tone scales called "gypsy." These will be discussed further in Chapter VIII.

Sergei Prokofiev's life was also touched by Scriabin. In 1910 he dedicated his orchestral composition, *Dreams*, "To the composer who began with *Rêverie*," referring to that 1898 Conservatory miniature which was Scriabin's first realized attempt at the orchestra after the Concerto (not counting the ill-fated Arensky Scherzo).

Prokofiev may have once called Scriabin's Concerto "lackluster" and declined to play it. (Goldenveizer had also turned down a similar request, saying that his appearance would be too soon after the composer's own.) But Prokofiev was for a while enmeshed in Scriabin as Miaskovsky was in Glazunov. Prokofiev reduced the *Divine Poem* for piano, and wanted to show it to Scriabin personally, but lost his nerve, thus never meeting him. On his graduation from the Petersburg Conservatory in 1909, the board had agreed that he and the other composition students in general were "all bent on becoming Scriabins." Later, Prokofiev would say that "Scriabin cannot have disciples. He must stand alone. He is a solitary genius." Still, on Scriabin's death, Prokofiev played a memorial evening of Scriabin's music in St. Petersburg, and in 1918 when he made his début as pianist in New York, he included Scriabin on the program. (So would Koussevitzky in his first conducting appearance with the Boston Symphony.)

Koussevitzky, with Scriabin in the piano role, gave the first performance of *Prometheus* on 2 March, 1911. They performed it without the *tastiera per luce*, not even a garland of Christmas lights. But it was a shattering evening of brilliance. Leonid Pasternak painted a portrait of the event and Koussevitzky bought it from him. One critic called *Prometheus* "the most original piece of contemporary music . . . a bridge between what *is* and what *will be*."

Safonov, who was in the audience, commented to his coterie, including Vera, "It offends the nose." He conducted it later, but perhaps without changing his mind.

Prometheus won the Glinka Prize of $750. (*Ecstasy* had won in 1908, but the amount was less, $350.) The Beliaeff committee awarding the prize had been opposed to *Prometheus*, but Scriabin's friend Liadov, as chairman, insisted. Kashperov wrote that the motive behind Liadov's unusual insistence was kindness and charity. It may have been, as Scriabin had broken with Koussevitzky and was once again in serious financial troubles. Liadov, himself, had misgivings. He truly thought the piece "insane," was totally unable to follow its musical abstractions, and expressed to his friends that no sooner had he signed the protocol document than he was seized with fears that next day Scriabin would be carted off to an asylum.

The quarrel with Koussevitzky was about money. When the "Russian Musical Edition" settled accounts in their annual fiscal statement in 1911, after the *Prometheus* performance, Koussevitzy showed a thousand rubles at Scriabin's earnings for the Volga tour the year before. This amount meant that he was being paid about $50 a concert. As usual between the two men, nothing had been put in writing, nor even discussed, since Scriabin hated financial transactions of any kind. (For sanitary reasons, as well as distaste, he would put on gloves before taking or giving money to a tradesman at the apartment door.)

Scriabin was insulted. "A scandal," he screamed, using one of his favorite words. (Some of the others were "nice," "minimum," "maximum," "principle.") "I even received a bigger fee when I was a student!" Koussevitzky, feeling that his $2,500 annual stipend justified the parsimony, said angrily, "You're not worth more," and sent Scriabin a bill for all monies so far advanced. Scriabin countered with a reckoning which deducted his usual rates for the various pieces the firm had published, including *Prometheus*.

The two men never spoke to each other again, and how Moscow gossips embroidered the story! Scriabin would not even utter his name, and used the initial "K" or said indirectly, "That man!" Koussevitzy continued to play Scriabin. Scriabinists, discussing the dispute, generally feel that Koussevitzky behaved stingily. The Koussevitzky faction considered that Scriabin had "mortified" him by treating him from the very beginning as a "mechanic," a purveyor of other people's creative genius, and not as "an artist in his own right."

Unfortunately, the letters Scriabin wrote on this issue to Koussevitzky have not become public, although one man in Russia today claims he has possession of them. There were some once, because Koussevitzky showed them to Yuri Engel, Scriabin's first biographer in Russia, in 1916. It was as if, Engel said, Koussevitzky wanted to prove that he was in the right in the altercation. Engel was unconvinced, for he was too much of a Scriabinist at heart. The Scriabin Museum has pressed for the release of the letters, but they quite probably no longer exist.

Even without Koussevitzky, Scriabin had other conductors for his music. Nikisch toured Russia again. Glazunov (a bad conductor by any standards) played Scriabin. And in December 1911, Rachmaninov and Scriabin appeared in public on the same platform: Rachmaninov leading Scriabin's First Symphony (without chorus), Scriabin playing his Concerto to Rachmaninov's bâton. "My only regret is that it is the Concerto and not *Prometheus* which reunites us," Scriabin wrote in accepting Rachmaninov's invitation and signifying accord as to the proposed fee, $350. But Rachmaninov the reactionary was unable to accept Scriabin the musical radical of *Prometheus*. Besides,

Koussevitzky and Scriabin had too recently performed it, and even played it in a pair of concerts in Berlin earlier.

By now, Scriabin had passionate adherents and propagandists among young, intelligent piano professors at various Conservatories throughout Russia—Matthew Pressman in Rostov on the Don, Glière in Kiev, Alexander Horowitz and Anatol Drozdov in Ekaterinodar, Bekleminshev in Kharkov.

The composer's silence of 1910, seen in the light of 1911, was a period of gestation. During the summer of 1911, at a rented summer house near Kashira outside Moscow, Scriabin drafted the Seventh Sonata Op. 64. Its first sketches show considerable variance in rhythm and in distribution of tones over the keyboard. He marked the tempo direction, "Prophetically." When Koussevitzky published it— the last Scriabin music under his imprint—he changed the word to *Allegro*. Later in the season, Scriabin worked out two "demonic" sonatas at the same time, the Sixth Op. 62 and the Ninth Op. 68.

In the autumn he finished the Sixth Sonata, although he declined to play it in concert. This pair of sonatas are each quite outside the areas of Scriabin's ecstatic, end-of-the-world esthetics so characteristic of his other works. This will be discussed further in Chapter IX.

Again, as in 1903, perhaps money was the reason which triggered such a burst of musical activity. Scriabin sent Koussevitzky some money toward the amount of work promised. Koussevitzky returned it, demanding compositions not coin.

Once the rift between the two men became common knowledge, Liadov wrote a letter begging Scriabin to return to the publishing house, for the sake of Belaieff's memory. Boris Jurgenson, head of an even older and equally lustrous publishing house for music, won Scriabin, offering him $3,000 a year—the most money he ever received from patron or publisher.

Meanwhile, until these negotiations were on paper in October, 1912, Alexander Siloti entered Scriabin's life as a conductor and friend, booking a double performance of *Prometheus* on the same program. The symphony was less difficult to apprehend after several hearings. Siloti also arranged for a wealthy patron, M. Tereshchenko, to send Scriabin private gratuities in the interim, although Siloti's own wife was a Tretyakov and very wealthy. She loved Scriabin more than Siloti did and in later years, it was she who kept his memory alive most vividly.

Legally, Scriabin had no right to appear with other conductors or to send his manuscripts to anyone except Koussevitzky. However there was nothing left to be done, except be spiteful. Koussevitzky brought Debussy to Russia in the autumn of 1913, and although every other foreign musician visiting Russia called on Scriabin, who was then the nation's leading composer with a huge international reputation, the two men were never introduced.

Professor Ivanovsky of the Kiev Conservatory once asked Debussy pointblank if he had not met Scriabin in Moscow. He had not. Scriabin heard Debussy conduct *La Mer*, and bought a copy of the miniature score, which he kept on his work desk along with Richard Strauss's *Ein Heldenleben*. Scriabin however, did not like in general "the passive musical language" of the impressionists. As history shows, for all his romanticism and subjectivity, he was closer to expressionism in technique. He called Debussy *par terre*, or "earthy." A worse term of opprobrium did not exist in Scriabin's vocabulary.

V Last Years

In October, 1912, Scriabin took the apartment where he was to die, and which has become the official Scriabin Museum as sanctioned by Lenin. He became increasingly withdrawn, less social despite his celebrity, and more and more surrounded by an exclusive circle of friends. The painter Alexander Golovin, a carry-over friend from Scriabin's theater-going year of 1910 (he did the sets for Diaghilev's production of *Firebird* and *Afternoon of a Faun*), described Scriabin at this period as "something of a puzzle, strange, one of those people whom one simply doesn't know how to reach . . . When he was in a good mood he was lively and an attractive conversationalist. But these moods were rare, it seemed."

Scriabin's party-giving now centered around deeply mystical princes and princesses; Count Alexi Tolstoi, the playwright; symbolist poets; hangers-on such as Alexei Podgaetsky (who emigrated after the Revolution and became well known in Germany as an actor-mime under the name of Chabrov); Alexander Brianchaninov, a reactionary Anglophile whose Theosophical convictions led him to start a movement to canonize Scriabin as a prophet. There were, of course, also musicians who accepted his music with alacrity and his ideas reluctantly. Nikolai Zhilaev, the composer and pedagogue, was expelled from the circle. He had once exclaimed, "Better to write sonatas," after Scriabin read one of his poetic texts. Tatyana, to the irritation of everyone, watched over the circle's privacy with officiousness.

In the summer of 1912, Scriabin went abroad to Switzerland for a rest from his extended concertizing. He and Willem Mengelberg had toured Holland and Germany with *Prometheus*, and he had given twelve concerts within the space of two months. He also composed the three Études Op. 65, and wrote about them in a postcard to Sabaneeff, "I salute you from the clouds of space. It is marvelous here . . . no music, only the cows produce art here—with their tinkling bells . . . I inform you of something . . . quite painful for all defenders of the faith: A composer you know has written three études! In fifths (Horrors!), in ninths (How depraved!) and in major sevenths (the last fall from Grace!?) What will the world say?" The world now says, unequivocally, that these last among his total of twenty-six études are among his most remarkable contributions to piano literature.

By January 1912, Scriabin put the Seventh Sonata in polished form and played it repeatedly in concert. He finished the Ninth Sonata in the summer of 1913. At this same time too, while summering in Aleksin, a small town on the banks of the Oka River (a particularly beautiful part of Russia full of woods with sweet-smelling earth and typically Russian with its especially brilliant sunshine), he quickly composed the Tenth Sonata, his most radiant and light-filled work. According to Delson, this was "his least subjective composition . . . least restricted by the dogma of monoharmony." Scriabin once described it as "expressing the impression of a forest." Biographer Mikhail Mikhailov, Professor at the Leningrad Conservatory, speaks of its "crystal clarity full of quiet and peace."

Scriabin had trouble with the Eighth Sonata Op. 66, begun earlier. It would be the last sonata, not the Tenth, which he would finish, and then not until autumn of 1913 back in Moscow. As with the Sixth, Scriabin never played the Eighth in public. He always said, much as he loved the Eighth, his last born, that he was unable to leave his other creative work long enough to bring it up to "concert level." He considered it the most difficult of all his compositions as far as performance was concerned.

In the summer of 1913, Scriabin also traveled to Lausanne to see his vacationing father and meet with the new additions to his family. He went without Tatyana, since the reconciliation to Scriabin's second marriage was not yet fully accomplished. The father remained moralistic and condemnatory in every sense. They visited his mother's grave in the Italian Alps where she had gone as a last measure to cure her tuberculosis. He wrote to Tatyana that he felt "complicated feelings . . . complicated, and for me, new feelings. But how? . . . If only I had told you the hour I would visit the grave, then you could have *seen* all that I experienced . . . I have suffered much these days, and the visit disquieted me. . . ."

Igor Stravinsky, ten years Scriabin's junior, made a point of calling on Scriabin that summer. He found the last sonatas "incomparable" as Scriabin played them for him (he had already studied the Seventh). But Stravinsky was startled and annoyed that Scriabin talked as if he had never heard his compositions. When Scriabin got around to *Petrushka* in 1914, he called it, dismissively, "busy."

As a youth, Stravinsky had chafed when his mother reproached him for not writing "like Scriabin." But the truth of the matter was that he did. As American conductor and Stravinsky amanuensis Robert Craft has pointed out, "A comparison of the *Poem of Ecstasy* with the *Firebird* reveals a debt far larger than is generally realized of one of the most popular to one of the least popular of early twentieth-century masterpieces." The famous "Petrushka chord" of two major triads separated by a tritone—C Major and F♯ Major combined, for example—is now seen to derive from Scriabin's harmonic system (as to be noted in Chapter VIII), and a fact which Scriabin overlooked when he was demolishing *Petrushka*.

In 1962, Stravinsky revisited Russia for the first time after the Revolution. He included on his itinerary a pilgrimage to the Scriabin Museum. He met there a young Russian composer who had made a tape filter to accompany a film called *Cosmic Space* based on Scriabin "ideas." Today, still, the Museum has become a meeting place for multi-media and electronic musicians, who do not find their experiments welcome in the conservative halls of Conservatories.

The flame of Scriabin's fame burned brightly. Ferruccio Busoni, visiting Russia, was charmed by Scriabin's Ninth Sonata. According to Alshvang, his pupil, Busoni kept all of Scriabin's sonatas constantly on his piano.

Under Alisa Koonen's influence, Scriabin composed the Two Dances Op. 73, subtitled "Dark Flame" (the "black fire" of ignorance in Theosophical terminology) and "Garlands," and also, what would prove to be one of his most popular and instantaneously effective piano-poems, "Toward the Flame" Op. 72. Here the flame is the center of the World Soul.

More and more, Brianchaninov (whose wife retained her maiden name and signed her formal letters "Her Serene

Highness Goncharova") substantiated Scriabin's already
colored thinking. Brianchaninov used the intimate form *ty*
with Scriabin, something not many others dared to do.
(Scriabin hated what he called *amikoshonstvo*, the friend-
liness of pigs, or "intimacy," and even in letters where he
might say "Dear Friend" or use first names he still signed
himself formally as "A. Scriabin.")

The two men spent three weeks in London in the spring
of 1914. Scriabin accepted the concert engagements there
with double purpose. He wanted to meet Annie Besant
and join the heart of the Theosophical Society. Besant hap-
pened to be in India, but Scriabin did dine with the secretary of the Society and even visited the woman in whose
arms Blavatsky had died. England was indispensable for
his and Brianchaninov's plans to go to India, where the
"Mysterium" with its high-frequency music now would
have to be performed.

Scriabin eagerly read the writings of yogi Ram Charak,
then in fashion. He took yogic breathing exercises, although he reproached Ram Charak for being too rational-
istic. "He wants to explain to Europeans of intelligence.
That's his teacher's task. But he endangers somewhat the
original Hindu relationship of man to the world." When
Scriabin was seriously undergoing yogic training, he said to
Sabaneeff, "It will give me remarkable powers. We don't
know how to breathe, nor eat nor sleep. In fact, we don't
even know how to live. We learn such stupid things in
school, and don't touch on importances. In Indian schools,
it's just the opposite. In the first grade, they learn to cul-
tivate the soul. . . . meditation, memorization . . . We
must have physical health in order to be able to control our
bodies wisely. I must, must, must live as long as possible."
He resumed his breathing exercises in front of Sabaneeff.
"Quite another feeling when you breathe with these

thoughts in mind," he said, "You know, I can hold my breath already for three minutes." Sabaneeff adds, "He showed me, but stopped midway."

Scriabin studied Sanskrit in order to find a base on which to construct a new language for his "Mysterium" text. He bought a white suit and a sun helmet. That summer, he spent hours working in the sunshine to accustom himself to India's tropical climate.

In England, Scriabin played his Concerto and *Prometheus* with Sir Henry Wood as well as two additional recitals. "Scriabin conquered England," Brianchaninov reported in his magazine, *New Link*. Most of intellectual London was converted patently to the idea that Scriabin was unusual and exciting. The critics were milder in their enthusiasm. Professor Charles Mayer of Cambridge University interviewed Scriabin and wrote a paper on his ability to hear colors.

However, during most of the hubbub in England, Scriabin was ill. A pimple had developed on his upper lip under his right mustache, and was incredibly painful. An English doctor lanced it. Scriabin made his début moving like an automaton.

With plans to go to India completed, Scriabin returned to Russia cancelling all next year's commitments. He feared that he would need a complete rest after the exploratory trip to India. He plunged himself into writing the text of a preliminary "Mysterium," which he now titled the "Prefatory Action," calling it a "general rehearsal for the 'Mysterium.'" The text contains new words such as "loveness" and "joying." One extraordinary line consists almost entirely of the syllables *"trop," "trup,"* and *"kryt,"* and means ominously, "We on covered trails covered with corpses." His friends joked behind his back that this was the "Harmless 'Mysterium,'" that is, its music would not dissolve the world in an abyss of flames. Less friendly acquaintances wondered if this ultimate composition which was to unite the world, not merely India, Russia, England, but everyone in the brotherhood of man, was to include Vera.

The outbreak of World War I, in the hot, rainless summer of 1914, stunned Scriabin not only by its tragedy, but as an example of the world-shaking battles already taking place in the astral atmosphere to which his "Prefatory Action" and "Mysterium" were central.

Scriabin rescued Tatyana's aunts from Belgium, and heard of the German atrocities. He reacted by saying, "War strips false civilization from man, and shows a nation's true being . . . You can see the bestiality of the Germans when you listen to Richard Strauss' music . . . This business isn't limited to war. After the war, enormous changes are going to come, changes of a Socialist nature. China and India will rise up. Africa will awaken . . . In the next few years we will live a thousand years."

Simultaneously with writing the text of the "Prefatory Action," he jotted down sketches for the music with different colored pencils—black, red, blue, violet. He pasted two pieces of ordinary score paper together in order to have enough staves on which to write the massiveness of the music—seventy lines, not the usual thirty he used in *Prometheus* which was, indeed, already grandiose enough.

The idea of the "Prefatory Action" gradually grew larger. In addition to colored lights, processions, and scents, he wanted tastes to accompany the music. (What would Rimsky have said to that?!) A chorus was to declaim his text. They would be specially garbed in "a symphony of flavors . . . a costumed symphony," he elaborated. They would whisper and make rustling sounds. The members of the orchestra would also participate in the motions and movements, not just sit as they do in concerts and operas.

"That would be awful," he said, "They must almost dance
. . . participate in the action . . . play their instruments
as if they feel the sensation of each sound, as if caressing
each tone." When Scriabin talked this way, his friends
thought of what was sometimes said of his concerts, "Flow-
ers bloom under his fingertips as he plays."

He began planning for a special school to teach the singers and orchestral players to dance. He would be the
"preacher and teacher" of this school, as he would ultimately be the conductor of the "Prefatory Action" performance in India. He thought England would be the best
place for the school, since that country had been so re-
sponsive to the ideas behind *Prometheus*. He rather ambiv-
alently bridled that its mysticism, more than its music,
had appealed to the English public. He also worried about
his most mystical friends being the most "lifeless in coun-
tenance." He meant Branchaninov and Podgaetsky.

He began to hate concertizing even more. "It's not my
business now," he said, because public appearances took
time and attention away from the "Prefatory Action." His
right hand hurt again, as it had during his Conservatory
days. "I am an invalid," he complained. "I'll be a disgrace
today," he sometimes said before a concert, begging for
sympathy, although these remarks sound more like pre-
concert nervousness. "How hateful all this is, these public
appearances. I wasn't made for it. I'm simply not a pianist.
. . ." During intermissions, he would grieve to his friends,
"Nothing is coming out today . . . it's like a wall. I'm
not feeling what I must. . . ." But Alexander Ossovsky
and Rachmaninov attended Scriabin's last concert on 2
April, 1915. They agreed that Scriabin played "with unusual inspiration and emotional penetration."

Vladimir Horowitz was taken to Scriabin for "appraisal,"
much as Scriabin himself had been produced before Anton

Rubinstein. As Horowitz remembers the story, Scriabin advised a general musical education. "Make him a cultured musician, not a sectarian," he said, meaning for the child not to develop into a virtuoso specialist. Artur Rubinstein also appeared before Scriabin, but Scriabin grew sharp with him as soon as he said he did not want to be an exclusive Scriabinist ("sectarian," it would seem). He wanted to play Brahms, Beethoven and other composers antipathetical to Scriabin. Still, Rubinstein gave the first performance of the Fifth Sonata in London soon after.

Scriabin much preferred his special circle of friends to any socializing or obligation of passing judgment on upcoming musicians. He enjoyed his long talks with Mozer, was fascinated with the discovery of radioactivity, instantly accepted "the crisis of Euclidean geometry and Newtonian mechanics" and the emergence of "a many-measured space." The years from 1900 to 1913 had opened windows wide over the world—Max Planck's quantum theory, Einstein's relativity, Nils Böhr's theory of atomic structure. "Yes, you see," Scriabin said to Mozer, "this is all the failure of our materialistic natural sciences."

And in the arts abroad, Braque and Picasso had started cubism. Proust had published the first volume of Swann. "What was art then in Russia?" Pasternak once asked in speaking of the pre-World War I period. "It was the young art of Scriabin, Blok, Komissarzhevsky . . . It was so forward-looking, so gripping and original, and it was so astonishing." Scriabin was indeed at the heart of Russia's world of music, poetry, and theater. . . . and science?

He made some fifty-five pages of music notes and sketches for the "Prefatory Action." (Persons of a mystical twist may find significance in that number: Scriabin's published music lacks any Op. 55). On the basis of these sketches, the young Soviet composer Alexander Nemtin has reconstituted the "Prefatory Action," somewhat as Charles Koechlin recreated Debussy's ballet score, *Khamma*, or as Franco Alfano completed Puccini's *Turandot*. Conductor Kyril Kondrashin, himself a pupil of Zhilaev, has scheduled for 1974 performances of this fabricated, invented work for chorus, soloists and orchestra, based on jottings.

The "Prefatory Action" was to have taken place originally with the Himalayas as background—the Theosophists in London recommended Darjeeling to Scriabin—and incorporate sunrises and sunsets as part of the décor. The text divides into explanatory and descriptive groupings: There are waves, representing currents of life, sunbeams, mountains, meadows, forests and deserts. These choral groupings imply life's manifold multiplicity in the one spiritual, invisible Unity. Scriabin often said that when he saw nature, he felt a matching "process of energy" inside himself, and that natural phenomena were external expressions of his internal reality.

The "Prefatory Action" begins with a bass soloist intoning the plot of the work. Calling himself "the Pre-Eternal," that which was before the beginning, he announces that the Infinite will descend into the Finite, Spirit will infuse Matter, and that the ecstasy of love will be enacted. This is stated over a shimmering tremolo chord of many notes, considerably more complex than the six-note chord on which *Prometheus* was based. In the sketch books there is one extraordinary thirteen-note chord comprising three major dominant seventh chords over a root tone of F. The chord is spelled F, D, F♯, A, C♯, F, A, C, E, A♭, C, E♭, G. The major dominant sevenths are D, F♯, A, C♯; A, C♯, E, A♭ (G♯); C♯, F (E♯) A♭ (G♯), C (B♯).

Establishing enormous complexity at the outset, Scriabin wanted to unfold his principle that, as he often explained in various ways, "Complexity is the path to simplicity."

Elsewhere in the "Prefatory Action," Scriabin wanted sheer "two-tone harmonies . . . even unisons."

In between trumpet fanfares, the chorus chants a passage descriptive of the birth of the Universe, a collision of galaxies, worlds, planets, stars, and from this struggle Eternity, as opposed to the Pre-Eternal, is born. The Father, a preextant "God," marries "Sister Death"—a pale vision. Death symbolizes "endlessness" and the Indian concept of the suspension of time in eternity. Her appearance is accompanied by the slow, contemplative music which Scriabin published as Prelude Op. 74 No. 2. On another occasion, he used this same music to describe the "desert" theme.

The male and female principles of the world, as we know them, issue from their union separately as tenor and contralto. The woman describes herself: "In the white flame I am the incandescent diamond/ I am the ineffable bliss of dissolution/ I am the joy of death." The male asks to be led to her. "Hear my prayer and reveal to me the mystery of Death," he sings. She explains, "Life with its delusions, agonizing dreams," is a series of "multicolored spaces dividing us/ Amid the wondrous radiance of star-bloomed adornments. To enthrall me, you must pass through them, overcome them." The Female Principle now becomes Death and coaxes him to her—"You must see the light, hear your prophetic dream . . . I am not, when you are there . . . only you exist, you fill everything from yourself."

The Woman demands three sacrifices, the first being that he must make love to her. This equation of sex and death, familiar from Wagner's love-death fixation, and perhaps too from the French language which calls the orgasm "la petite mort," had appeared before in Scriabin's thinking, as in Freud's. In Scriabin's notebooks, after ecstatic references to love, sorrow instantly emerges. In his opera, the final, culminative act of love ends in the fiery

immolation of the lovers and the world around them. Their
duet there and in the "Prefatory Action," announces love-
making, death, and world's end.

A dancing chorus of women enters, "shimmering and
froth, illumining and sound," as if to prepare the marriage
of Man with Death. A chorus of men sings antiphonally.
Seven angels arrive representing children of the union:
"Builders of the world . . . They are warriors against
God, destroyers of walls . . . They are the constructors
of a radiant cathedral/ In which the drama of the Universe takes place," the text oratorically explains. As the
Male-Female union takes place, the Woman explains the
duality of love, "I enthralled you, but soon I shall be in
your thrall/ In your wreath I will be a wondrous star. . . ."

Further multiplicity—as multitudes form a scattering
world—comes with the Waves of Life, born out of mankind's need to "differentiate," to "distinguish," to analyze
and break down the unity of the original synthesis. Here
is the I and Not-I separation of all finite "things," matter
and material. The waves are impelled by a single current,
which flows outward from Eternity down into Humanity—
"Down from transparency/Toward a stony gloom." Between the waves, there is an additional erotic scene. "The
tender delight/ Of touching for the first time/ The mysterious sweetness/ Of moist lips kissing/ The sweet moan-
ing . . . by amorous lights. . . ."

The waves are encased in the raiment of their bodies,
and they enact a gamut of human feelings ". . . all the
more torturing, lovely, sensuous and corporeal." There is
laughter, weariness, supplication, and solution: "You gain
knowledge of yourself through tales told by fractured sunbeams," and "A sunbeam dropped in a lightning cloud/
Above the longing wave." The wave soars toward the sunbeam. There is a "sacred instant of creation, blessed instant,

fiery instant." It is no more than "the reflection—pale, white and fatal—of Death."

Through the varying acts of love, more and more of the universe is created. The mountains describe themselves as "The frozen impulses of amorous rage, the petrified billows of stormy caresses." The forests call themselves "Twilight cathedrals" into which all creatures pour "mysterious, langorous lights." The deserts are the "kisses of sunbeams on the earth." And with the same words he used to describe the Tenth Sonata to Sabaneeff, the world of insects is born —"I am a winged caress." Lepidoptera transform themselves into "savage lacerating beasts . . . writhing crawling snakes." But the "winged caress" remains the "I" of the voluptuous One, darling of the "moist elements."

Curiously, as Scriabin was writing about Death, death arrived. His life had been a series of victories over peaks of obstacles. The impetus of his enthusiasm and flight was to overcome life's torment, and to invent his own supraterrestial reality. Death seemed to be the only remaining hindrance between his total compass of the world. The "Prefatory Action" and the "Mysterium" dispose of this ultimate mystery of mysteries, life's most unanswerable question. And death overtook this boldest of his speculations. He even seemed to anticipate his final illness, in a somewhat atypical lessening of his megalomania a few weeks before he fell ill. "Individuality is a precious vessel from which the One drinks the knowledge of suffering and joy. I am only the vessel," he said to a friend.

On 4 April, 1915, the London pimple returned. On 7 April, he felt ill. His temperature rose drastically to 106 degrees. On 11 April, Moscow's leading specialists were called in, and incisions in Scriabin's face had to be made. His beloved Dr. Bogorodsky, a member of the mystic inner sanctum around Scriabin, was unable to cut his patient's face. On 12 April, there was another doctor and more incisions. Unaccountably, the pimple had turned into a carbuncle, then into a furuncle, streptococcus staphylococcus blood poisoning and bacteremia. A massive distribution of infection spread throughout Scriabin's body. On 13 April he said his last words: "But this pain is unbearable . . . This means the end . . . But this is a catastrophe!" And in the middle of the night, he shouted out, "Who's there?"

"But this is a catastrophe!" has been interpreted generally as a sign of megalomania, as if he meant that it would be a catastrophe for the world, if he was not allowed by life to finish the "Prefatory Action." It seems more likely that the remark expressed his catastrophic realization that he was dying. Scriabin's admirers were badly shaken by his untimely death. What would his future music have been like?

Here was a man who had composed for scarcely twenty-five years. His compositions for piano number around two hundred, and for orchestra, less than a dozen. His entire lifetime of sound can be heard in little more than twelve hours of listening.

The funeral was the most fashionable event in Moscow in years. The Kremlin choir sang a mass for the dead. Rachmaninov, Taneyev and the uncles were pallbearers for the coffin. There was an endless number of wreaths. Koussevitzky sent one, while his brother composed a sonnet for one of the newspapers. All-night vigils were held, and four days after his death, Scriabin's corpse was escorted to the burial ground. Ellen von Tiedebӧhl, the German correspondent who had accompanied the Volga tour, reported the final interment for *Metronome* in New York.

"Among the immense crowd was seen a large number of young people, who, with linked hands made a chain along the procession, singing the Russian anthem for the dead, ending with the impressive words, 'Eternal memory to him!' "

For weeks the papers were full of obituaries. Composer Miaskovsky called the death, "Terrible . . . and just as absurd as the War itself." Even those artists, poets, actors and musicians who had resented Scriabin for saying, "All is my creation. The world is the activity of my consciousness. All that exists, exists only in my awareness. All is *my* activity," knew full well that he had, after all, lived in a world of people, places, and things. Even those who had spurned his questing ideas for supertruths felt that something in the system of things, in world order, had gone awry and would remain askant and askew. Only today would it seem that the pieces of the puzzle—the enigma of Scriabin—are beginning to fall into place.

Of all the many thousands of words written about Scriabin, one memoir depicts him in the last month of his life and, possibly, describes how he would most like to be remembered. He is walking in the Dmitrov Chaussée park with Apollon, his seventeen-year-old half-brother. Apollon has recently fallen off a tram injuring his hand, and one finger is in splints. He thinks he has lost his chances of becoming a musician. Apollon writes:

> This was our last conversation and I remember every detail of it. He said he could express any idea, experience or appearance of nature in music. The "language of music" is limitless as it is with life and nature. He was absorbing musical ideas, nuances, from everything around us. Afraid he would forget something, he jotted everything down in his little notebook, like a stenographer taking notes in a code which only he understood.

Our walk was reaching an end. It was close to evening. We came to a bridge over a brook and he looked at it for a long time. An automobile passed by and stirred up a lot of dust and a flight of birds. Scriabin began answering me distractedly. Suddenly he took out the little book again and began writing with his pencil. This lasted several minutes. Then he began to sing and make gestures and nod his head to some rhythm.

We returned home quietly, as he was plunged in thought. He explained in time that he had notated in music all our feelings of that afternoon—our conversation, the moments standing on the bridge, the car, the sound of the flight of birds.

"You know, Lyusha, I have noted and will make music out of your personal distress and the sensations in today's experience. I will tell you when the piece is published . . . Just think, I can paint a better picture in music than a good painter can ever paint of *my* music."

VI   *Mysticism*

True as it might be that understanding the full meaning of the lyrics can destroy the experience of a song, a grasp of the mysticism, philosophy, content or program behind a piece of Scriabin's music cannot but enhance. What Scriabin intended by his life standpoint, and how this intention is received are two entirely different matters. The message may be accepted or rejected, enjoyed or greeted with revulsion. Certainly, Scriabin's mysticism was and is irrational. The schizophrenic, the mystic and the artist meet at some dangerous connecting point, and psychosis and transcendence are sometimes difficult to sort or separate. I say this in the face of today's "occult revival" and the widespread diaspora of believers in those "things unseen" dwelling in that place beyond our three dimensions. "From the point of light within the mind . . . let light descend on earth," states the Rainbow Family invocation. It could be Scriabin speaking instead of a contemporary religious youth cult in America. In short, the believer has no questions and the non-believer, no answers.

However, we should not, I think, follow the recom-

mendation of Soviet musicologist, Sergei Pavchinsky, who
voices an official view:

> Scriabin's heroic and lyrical music has earned its "citizen's
> rights." We must reexamine those aspects which the com-
> poser himself regarded as mystical. The fact of the matter is
> that Scriabin as a great artist unhesitantly used the feelings
> associated with the real world. His commentaries and re-
> marks on many of his compositions are full of weird and
> fantastic images. But they all retain a connection with the
> magnificence of nature . . . As a consequence of the expres-
> siveness of Scriabin's music, he shows how it pushes away
> from a realistic succession of picturizations. This is why, re-
> gardless of the indications of the composer, we accept his
> "mysticism" as contemplation of nature's greatness, as pic-
> tures of cosmic colors, the acceptance of which enriches the
> spiritual life of man. It must be emphasized that "cosmic
> emotions" are not necessarily tied to mysticism or an ideal-
> istic world-view. No need to succumb to the pretty feelings
> of the mystic.

Nor do we need to follow Pavchinsky—and we will not
in Chapter VIII—when he asserts that a "complicated system" of analysis fails to "clear up the real basis for Scriabin's harmonies."

The *fons et origo* of music was religion, philosophy, and
by extension, mysticism—the transmission of sound in spirit.
The word "mystic" comes from the Greek *myecin*, "close
to the lips or eyes," meaning that mystics see innermost
truths which are inaccessible to the naked eye and heart
of the positivist. The mystic bends the world to himself as
he thinks or dreams it rather like the creative artist himself.
On the other hand, the realist, or scientist, must demonstrate and prove what he knows, before it can be called
"real." The two opposite poles have, in our time, grown

somewhat closer. As physics and the exact sciences advance more and more "unthinkable propositions" and bring about their actuality, so too have mysticism's unthinkable assertions, such as the power of mind over matter, rebirth, predestination, other worlds, the blur of all sensory and extra-sensory phenomena, become less preposterous.

The oldest of the Hindu Holy Books, the Rigveda, consists of sung hymns. Scriabin venerated these from afar and by hearsay since they were not translated at that time. By 500 B.C. Indian religious philosophers, the grammarians, had built an entire system of thought based on sound, *sphota*, the imperishable substratum of sound in the universe. *Sphota* was considered to be the Brahman itself, the Absolute, the Supreme Being, Supreme Reality, Supreme Truth, knowledge of which alone gives liberation. From *sphota* emanated "meaning," and after this the objective world as we see, feel, smell and hear it was created by *sphota's* vibration.

The mysteries of ancient Greece, too, were unimaginable without music. "Holy men today are ignorant magicians, having forgotten their magic," Scriabin said. He believed that originally the Egyptians and Greeks, and of course the Hindus, had powers which modern man had allowed to atrophy. His purpose in music was to rekindle those powers. According to Scriabin, there was simply no illogic about Amphion building the walls of Thebes by charming stones into place with his flute's music. He was unquestioning of Orpheus with his lyre stilling savage beasts and making trees dance in the wind to their own aeolian harp. (He was silent on the subject of Orpheus being torn to pieces by the women of Thrace for refusing to give his autograph, but he was punctilious about giving his to strangers who asked, since he thought it a "Western custom.")

Plato was incontestable, Scriabin believed, when he described the ideal world as a place where everything shines, and where fire is "most beauteous." After all, the Bible, and Scriabin in his youth had read *Ezekiel*, describes the Garden of Eden as being "filled with stones of fire." Scriabin accepted Plato's contention that the stars in the heavens were the gods in perceptible form, that they communicated with each other by means of flickering lights instead of speech. Making music a materialization of the occult in sound and a restoration of magical powers so common in antiquity (according to myth and legend), was left for Scriabin to accomplish. Or so, at least, he thought.

While those Mysteries of Greece also used added excitants, Scriabin did not. He thought that music, with its remarkable sounds stretching back through the centuries, eons, eternities, and manvantaras to touch the original and all-generative *sphota*, was sufficient. Those *poisons sacrées* (substances to induce visions) were, for instance, the alcohol of Dionysian orgies in honor of Bacchus, or hallucinogenic mushrooms of the Eleusinian Mystery near Athens, where Demeter and Persephone were worshiped as goddesses of "fruitful soil" or symbols of man's fruitfulness in the erotic act. To Scriabin, these were "coarse" means and ways to reproduce spiritual realities.

Scriabin described his projected symphonies of colors, touches, aromas (he even began a tone-poem called "Icarus" which incorporated an airplane propeller in the orchestra; one time in an after dinner conversation, he toyed with the idea of a "counterpoint" of pain which would transmute a toothache into music), as "having no roots in the present day arts of our race as we know it." He told Sabaneeff that his ultimate music belonged to those "theurgic arts of lost, ancient, mystic cultures." He said that man's psyche needed to be shaken by what he called, "a hypnosis of apparitional rhythms." Art as magic, in other words. Sound, shifting

lights, the play of gestures, triumphal processions, sacerdotal dances, billowing scents, touching caresses, ritualistic
and exorcistic prayers, light and church lamps, smoking
incenses and perfumes, genuflections and kisses, all combined "to cross the abyss of thousands of centuries," he
said to Sabaneeff. Together, they created "the holy mysticism of all cultism." One might add, "all occultism," too.

Scriabin was very clear. He said to Sabaneeff, and the
gist of his words has been corroborated by other contemporaries, "I cannot understand how to write *just* music now.
How boring! Music, surely, takes on idea and significance
when it is linked to a single plan within a whole view of
the world. People who just write music are like performers
who just play an instrument. They become valuable only
when they connect with a general idea. The purpose of
music is revelation. What a powerful way of knowing it
is!" Put another way, as a Chinese painter of the eleventh
century said, similarly, "The wise man creates with the
help of his spirit, and thereby has the same active force of
heaven and earth."

Reporters and interviewers bothered Scriabin with requests for enlightenment as to what his music meant. His
stock answer was, "Most of my musical poems have a specific psychological content, but not all of them need program notes." There was a time in 1905, after the *Divine
Poem* and in the midst of the *Poem of Ecstasy*, when Scriabin wrote a friend that he was concerned with matters
"other than music," and it looked as if his mysticism would
overwhelm the musical aspects of his creative talents. He
also often said to friends he fully realized that in order to
persuade the public to his ideas as a mystic, he had first to
"subdue" them with music, which was one reason why he
concertized.

But he was never cavalier as to the necessity for explana-

tory "texts," as he called the poems accompanying his
music. In 1907, when he invited Alfred Laliberté, who had
written him a fan letter, to New York, he searched everywhere in his papers looking for the poem to the Fourth
Sonata, since it "explains better than my words." He
could not find it, so he said he would "show" it to
Laliberté when he arrived. In another letter to Laliberté,
from Brussels in May in 1909, inviting him again to visit
him, he wrote, "When you are here I will bring you up to
date regarding many things, I will tell you about my artistic projects and a thousand happenings which can't help
but interest you. But if you don't come, you will know
nothing. Wicked boy!!!" (And he warned him against
sugar, since Laliberté was already too fat.)

Another time when Scriabin was deep in working out
the scheme of the *Poem of Ecstasy*, he found himself writing a text to it. He described his astonishment to Tatyana.
"I have just written a monologue with the most divine
word colors. The very meter of the words kindles the
meaning of the poem. I am expressing what will be one
and the same as the music."

Later, he regarded the poem to the *Poem of Ecstasy*
much as a book of the Bible is considered "instructional"
and the theological basis of a world concept. A widely
quoted sentence from Scriabin's letter of 1907 to Nikolai
Artsybushev, the lawyer-composer and business manager
of the Belaieff firm and chairman of its Board of Direc-
tors, reads: "I am thinking of not printing the text with
the score. Conductors who want to play the *Poem of
Ecstasy* can always be apprized that it has one. But in general, I would prefer for them to approach it first as pure
music." But this is only part of the story. The rest of the
letter reads, "What do you think about this? Besides, if
you insert the text then it must be translated into French

at the very least. My wife is working on this now, but I doubt that she will be able to finish it so quickly."

In 1906, earlier, he had written to Felix Blumenfeld about the *Divine Poem*. "I am very sorry that I didn't know you were performing my symphony. I would have sent the explanatory text. You probably know that it was written with a philosophical program." The program notes printed at the time of Nikisch's performance in Paris were a "condensation," in Scriabin's words, of a longer, now lost poem. In his famous letter of self-explanation requested by Nikolai Findeisen, editor of the *Russian Musical Gazette*, dated 13 December, 1907, Scriabin said, "I cannot inform you of my ideas in a few words. I will say only that as far as content goes, the *Poem of Ecstasy* serves as a little hint of what I want to present in my main composition [the "Prefatory Action" and "Mysterium"]. Its text, in turn, requires a commentary which I may publish separately."

In a later letter to Artsybushev, Scriabin is more emphatic. "I am very eager to have the brochure of the *Poem of Ecstasy* sold in the lobby. In all probability Jurgenson has the brochure, since I've discussed this matter with him. Be so kind as to let me know about this. If need be, I myself can send you several hundred copies of it." (Scriabin had privately printed five hundred copies of the poem, as well as the Fifth Sonata and "Enigma" and "Dance of Languour.")

And to Modest Altschuler, who was to give the première of the *Poem of Ecstasy* in New York in 1908, he wrote, "I will send you a short résumé of the *Poem*, and I ask you to translate it into English. Best give it to Johnston. I think he'll do it for you and Yakov [Altschuler's brother] with pleasure. Be sure to put these remarks in the program. It will help somewhat explain the content of the *Poem* to listeners. You're going to have many troubles, my poor one, during rehearsals! The score is ten times more complicated than the third symphony." Earlier, when Scriabin was in America with Altschuler, they had worked together to translate the subtitle of the *Divine Poem's* middle movement—*Naslazhdeniya*. They agreed on "Ecstasies."

Mysticism dominated Scriabin's music. The Seventh Sonata is written, for example, on two "planes" simultaneously—the temporal (human) and supernal (mystical), as we will see in Chapter IX (p. 180). Scriabin developed a series of mystico-musical symbols as well. The descending leap of the minor ninth interval signified to him the "descent of spirit into matter." The alternating whole tone step up and down suggested the breathing in and out of Brahma, the Creator of the World and the god who first issued from the Brahman. A descending half-step embodied human sorrow.

Scriabin was fascinated by the mystical aspect of Russian bells, *zvon*, which means simply "sound." The bell, with its natural tuning, sharp overtones, and endlessly evaporating decibels, recaptures tensionless *sphota* more affectingly than perhaps any instrument. Temples, shrines, or churches without bells in some form are almost non-existent anywhere in the world. Religious services utilize their sound as an aid to producing heaven on earth, just as incense is the symbolic vehicle which conveys man's prayers here on earth upward to the gods or God above. Certainly, the sound of the bell absorbs the listener's mind and soul, and tangibly demonstrates the many or multiplicity as being within the one sound or unity. This was one of Scriabin's intellectual crochets, and unity within multiplicity, or diversity out of sameness, pursued Scriabin as idea as relentlessly as he pursued it as goal.

Bells hold enormous significance for Russians. As the American authority on Russian music, Boris Schwarz, points out, they are at once "joyous, ominous, alarming and beautiful," part of the gamut of emotions the spirit or soul must pass through before the final attainment of ecstasy. There is an old Russian phrase for being misinformed— "hearing the bell, he didn't know where he was," meaning that bells can transport a person until he loses his bearings or takes leave of his senses.

Scriabin's music, too, makes use of clangorous bell-like climaxes, the Seventh Sonata for instance. As the Tenth is called the "Trill Sonata," the Sixth could easily be dubbed the "Bell Sonata." Koussevitzky had to order specially made chimes, so as to let the climactic bells of *Prometheus* pierce the air thickened by the dense orchestration. And, as noted earlier, Scriabin wanted the bells of the "Prefatory Action" suspended from clouds high over the Himalayas, summoning the spectators from all over the world. Outlandish and unfeasible as an idea? Yes, but perhaps less so, when the zeppelin was invented shortly after Scriabin had conceived his idea. So Russians at the time said.*

For all the contumely heaped on Scriabin for his "dimestore" mystical hocus-pocus, conductor Robert Craft cites "young listeners today" finding in the coda of the *Poem of Ecstasy* (the beginning *sostenuto* marked *maestoso*, page 176 of the partitur) "a species of psychedelic exaltation." Hermann Hesse, another revived and resurrected god of the young, describes in *Steppenwolf* the mystical area where music resides very much as Scriabin would: "All we who ask too much and have a dimension too many could

* In this connection, as well as various experiments in overtone tuning for the performance of Scriabin's music (see Chapter VII, p. 136), it is interesting to mention that James Lawson, carilloneur of the Riverside Church in New York City, has performed the bell theme of the "Prefatory Action" on his carillon, as well as adapting "Mask" Op 63 No. 1 for the performance of Scriabin's music (see Chapter VII, p. n), it is piece for carillon, "Brightstar," in Scriabinesque style, which he dedicated to the composer's memory on 25 December, 1970.

not contrive to live at all if there were not another air to breathe outside the air of this world, if there were not eternity at the back of time; and this [music] is the kingdom of truth."

Surprisingly, few musicians have concretized their spiritual convictions in the spirit of their music. However, once the connection with religion, if not mysticism, was more commonplace. Bach composed music which was either "sacred" (the masses, for example) or "profane" (the dance tunes). Both served the greater good of *gloria in excelsis deo*. Scriabin's bursts of manic composing fervor were far from unique. Haydn described how he "wept tears of ecstasy" in the process of composing *The Creation*. "I could not have made it myself. It was not *I* who produced it," he insisted, which reminds one of Scriabin's "HE."

Down-to-earth Mozart spoke of his experience of seeing a whole piece of music *"wie ein einziger Laut"* (as a single sound), a transfixion which Scriabin well knew and described in Theosophical terms as placing himself *"sur le plan de l' unité"* (in that plane where all is one and the same, unified). And Scriabin certainly would have agreed with Beethoven when he remarked, "Religion and the art of playing the figured bass are one. No one can dispute this." Or again, when Beethoven wrote to a friend, "When I open my eyes I find myself involuntarily sighing, because what I see around me is so against my religion. I must despise this world which does not understand how music is a higher revelation than all other wisdom or philosophy."

The blur between musical interest and philosophical studies has existed for a long time now, ever since the philosopher-musicians of antiquity. Tchaikovsky recognized Schopenhauer as his intellectual mentor. Rimsky-Korsakov followed Spinoza. Wagner and Nietzsche enjoyed and suffered a friendship that rocked all Europe for a while. More philosophers have been musicians than vice versa. Nietzsche composed an execrable "Hymn of Life" for chorus and orchestra and he also played tolerably well on the piano. Déscartes and Rousseau composed a few pieces. Sir William Herschel, a musician, discovered the planet Uranus. Schopenhauer played the flute and said that he could easily imagine "music being a world in itself," precisely a sentiment Scriabin echoed at various times in his life. As for mysticism, both musicians and philosophers at various times have proclaimed music's mysterious power over the soul of man and the elements surrounding him, tenets which give benchmarks to the mystic's measurements and his incredible assertions of fancy as fact.

However, Wagner with his magic potions, supernatural gardens of worldly temptations, fires which envelop gods of the Ur-past, and his intellectual unfolding of the profound ethic concealed in myths, still is depicting rather than conjuring up the experience itself, as Scriabin claimed he himself did. Strauss in *Death and Transfiguration*, say, or Schoenberg in *Transfigured Night*, attempted music as communion, rather than communication. So, too, Debussy in *Pelléas et Mélisande* freighted his score with symbolism and mystery. But there have been few specifically mystical composers such as Scriabin. Most of them have kept the heavily opiate, smokefilled, joss house atmosphere of mysticism outside the concert hall. Scriabin's closest counterparts are found not in music but in poetry with William Blake, or in painting with Nicholas Roerich.

We can cite Cyril Scott, who is implacably mystic, complete with spiritualistic séances and a habitus of mediums and astrological schedules. Perhaps the list can include Gustav Holst, because his most celebrated composition, *The Planets*, was written on an occult, zodiacal platform, and Olivier Messiaen, the French, Christian mystic, who makes all kinds of preternatural assertions and writes music derived from Scriabin, such as *Et Expecto Resurrectionem*

Mortuorum. There is also Alan Hovhaness, who incorporates into his music meditations and enlightenments of orientalia, namely, *The Mysterious Mountain* and *Silver Pilgrimage.*

In 1972, the Canadian Broadcasting Corporation contacted Rosemary Brown, the musical medium, who claims to be in touch with various musicians long dead to us, but still living to her in the spirit world. Scriabin dictated her a little piece which he called *"Moment d'Espoir."* It sounds exactly like very early, and very bad Rachmaninov. So much for Scriabin in the afterlife.

However, Scriabin still has an article devoted to him in the *Encyclopédie des Musiques Sacrées.* And Marina Scriabina is emphatic when she writes, "It does not matter what emotions, passions or sensations the artist experiences. Rather, what matters is the structure of his inner world, of that which represents for him the act of creation, of that which constitutes the essence of his *being* and his *doing* both at the same time . . . His [Scriabin's] thought and music sprang from a common spiritual source."

Scriabin in his secret notebooks confided ideas which were so private and expansive, so conceited and crazy that some of them he dared not express even to his closest friends or lovers. The reader wearies of the abuse of the personal pronoun, the incessant pendulum swing between strength and weakness, conviction and doubt, and the endless climaxes and recapitulations and réprises of the intellect to prove what simply cannot be, let alone be proven. Still, the notebooks, like Scriabin's thousand letters, tell an absorbing story of a man's innermost life of ideas.

Take these passages which have not been published in English before:

I give full flowering to each feeling, each search, each thirst.
I raise you up, legions of feelings, pure activity, my children.

I raise you, my complicated, unified feelings, and embrace all of you as my one activity, my one ecstasy, bliss, my last moment.

I am God.

I raise you up, and I am resurrected, and then I kiss you and lacerate you. I am spent and weary, and then I take you. In this divine act I know you to be one with me. I give you to know this bliss, too. You will be resurrected in me, the more I am incomprehensible to you.

I will ignite your imagination with the delight of my promise. I will bedeck you in the excellence of my dreams. I will veil the sky of your wishes with the sparkling stars of my creation.

I bring not truth, but freedom.

*   *   *

Already I have propounded the beginning of pure mathematics. There exists the concept of unity, the concept of repetition, and now the concept of two. Now we can answer the question why one and one are always two: I have so composed one with one, so as to give the name "two." Whenever I create one with one they add up to unit with unit and I call the result two and derive a numerical sum.

Thus the mathematical "law" is simply a condition through which I . . .

And here Scriabin tapers off into that axiom, "Mathematics is music for the mind; music is mathematics for the soul."

In every given moment I find myself somewhere and I experience something. Reality appears to me as multiplicity in endless space and time. Therefore my experience is the center of a sphere with an enormous, limitless radius. From one view of this world which is given me and therefore is my one consciousness, I can not leave the sphere. From the other

view (which is obvious to me), my individual consciousness
does not limit being and the other *individual consciousnesses*
which are enclosed in my individual consciousness and are
locked away, inaccessible to my observation. From one side,
respectfully argued, I should deny everything outside the
sphere of my consciousness, because I can affirm only my
own sensations. Reality is accorded me only in psychic experiences. All which I do not say, do not think, and do not
see, all this too is the activity of my consciousness. If it stops,
the world is demolished. From the other side, there is the
conviction in me (which could be groundless) that my individual consciousness is only a drop in the ocean of many
other spheres which are self-contained and separated from
each other. In order to resolve this contradiction, one must
better analyze oneself and answer the question: What *is* individual consciousness, and how is it *possible* and to what
extent is it isolated from other *individual consciousnesses?*
Are there not links which one can count? Is there no serious
foundation for asserting that there is an *outside world?*

*   *   *

Being is not something separate from the desire for life. It
is the very same desire but objectified. Wish is the inner aspect of being.

The nature of life (action) is desire for the other, the *one*
and *nothing else*. The consequence of desiring (experience)
creates time. Action is the surge or lift of life. Surge (activity) in the highest degree is ecstasy. Absolute being is
ecstasy. (*What awakens action?*)

The soul must exploit its creative ability (opposition),
that is, must intoxicate itself with creativity before it can
return to a state of peace.

The soul must desire absolute being, ecstasy. How is
ecstasy possible?

Ecstasy is the highest *rising of activity. Ecstasy is the summit.*

How is the highest surge of activity possible?

The conditions of activity:

In the existing order of things, *protest* and longing for the new order exist. But this is only a single rhythmic figure. In thought-form, ecstasy is the *highest synthesis. In the guise of feeling, ecstasy is the highest bliss. In the guise of space, ecstasy is the highest development and destruction.* Generally, ecstasy is the summit, the last moment, which comprehends the whole history of humanity as a series of appearances.

Time and space objectify this longing. Deep eternity and unending space are constellations around divine ecstasy illuminating it.

I can not experience something consciously, if at the same time I do not experience everything else unconsciously. The unconscious side of my creative work participates in all. The universe is an unconscious process of my own creativity. "Man" is my individual consciousness in objective form. The world is the sum of all other individualities existing within my unconscious.

*   *   *

All is my creation. But creation exists only in my creations. They are *identical with each other.* I am nothing. I am only what I create. All that exists, exists only in my awareness. All is my activity, which in turn is only that which my activity produces. Therefore, it is impossible to say that the world exists. The existence of concepts, the essence, completely fails to express what the world presents outside one's self. The world of time and space is the process of my creativity. Here the word process, as a concept of time, does not express what I want to say. The world is my creativity and it is only a world. One is related to another, and nothing more. Nothing exists, nothing is created, nothing is really accomplished: All is play. And this play is the highest of real realities. All is my free and sole activity. Nothing is outside it. And it is a game . . . .

Foolishly enough, Scriabin saw all this intellection and mental gymnastics as suitable for dramatization, as he had earlier in his 1903 opera. In 1908, at the time most of these extracts were written, he announced that he had begun "a work for the stage," and the text was being written. This was not his only mistake. The contents of the notebooks themselves err. Scriabin was never able to say with the self-awareness of the "decadent" symbolist poet Fyodor Sologub: "What fearsome freedom have I reached through magic!" Danilevich, in his monograph on Scriabin, concludes that "Scriabin considered himself 'free' from everything which chains other people. But it was a frightening freedom, and an imaginary one." He likens Scriabin of the notebooks to the man who determined to leave the prosaic world and climbed to the top of the highest mountain. Beneath him was an abyss. He had nowhere to go. And he lacked wings on which to fly.

Over the years, Scriabin's philosophy underwent certain changes, but it retained a curiously steadfast, almost monotonous consistency whose central ingredients were monomania, megalomania and mysticism, in the sense that the power of the mind is unlimited and all worldly manifestations are either subject to its control or even created by it. Curiously, the first poem Scriabin ever wrote, dating from the age of fifteen, contains the genesis of all his later escapism, as well as the visionary aspect of his ideation. He used this as a caption to his unfinished, posthumously discovered Ballade of 1887. (The music was later partially incorporated in the Prelude in E Minor Op. 11 No. 4.)

> Oh country of visions!
> How different from this life
> Where I have no place
> But there, I hear voices,

A world of beatitudinous souls
I see.

Independently of Indian or Greek thought, but highly
indebted to Fichte and Schopenhauer and Nietzsche, Scriabin's first formulations of his thought conceived the world
as a unity, a unity created by the will of a hero or Super-
man. The whole history of the universe and its mankind
within it was the result of this individual act of free will.
This conviction took root when Scriabin was twenty years
old, and it was essentially an atheistic point of view, as
Schloezer states in his biography. In Scriabin's projected
opera the hero has an aria in which he sings,

> The caressing lies of religion
> Lull me not
> Their gently shining clouds
> Dim not my reason.

As Scriabin's self-consuming solipsism intensified throughout his lifetime, he used the word "God" less and less, and
often denied the historical existence of Jesus. As Danilevich
points out in a reflective, retrospective article on Scriabin
in *Sovetskaya Muzyka* No. 1, 1972, "He did not want anyone, not even God! to usurp his prerogatives." As he
changed and expanded his theories, he adjusted—not to
accommodate God—but to be more "reasonable." So he
developed the concept of the world being "one" in origin,
one by its very nature, and that ultimate unity could only
be known at the end of existence. His formula became
three-fold: life, cosmos, man. These three phenomena flowered like the past itself, out of centuries and generations
of "dark beliefs" and the striving to lose oneself in bliss or
beatitude. . . . ecstasy.

Since the world was "one," he embraced demonism or satanism as a "contrast" to the light he sought; just as on his deathbed he would notice that the unendurable pain he was suffering was a contrast to the inner state of ecstasy he frequently and normally felt. His laurels cast shadows, and he incorporated them in his music. He began this evil coloration in his music with the "Satanic Poem" in 1903. In this piece, coincidentally, despite many prior anticipations, he openly exploited the dominant ninth chord with a lowered fifth (the measures before the réprise). This will be discussed in Chapter VIII. As time passed, he would occasionally, usually in immediate juxtaposition to his most "saintly" music, give himself over completely to fire and brimstone music, as seen in the Sixth and Ninth Sonatas. "Ironies" Op. 56, "Mask" and "Strangeness" Op. 63, and "Dark Flame" Op. 73 are also exemplary of his demonic moods. He even went so far as to accept the subtitle "Black Mass" for the Ninth Sonata.

It must be remembered that Black Masses were seriously practiced and believed in, in pre-Revolutionary, Rasputin Russia. Some members of Scriabin's circle carried on "devilish" experiments. Nikolai Shperling, the painter, while at the front shortly after the outbreak of World War I, drank the blood of the wounded and ate the flesh of soldiers freshly killed in action. All this was part of a spiritual exercise to study the effects on his soul. He told Scriabin about this, much to the composer's morbid interest.

As Alexander Blok, the poet, wrote in 1919 somewhat fuzzily, "All cultures, scientific and artistic, have something of the demon in them. And the more scientific, the more artistic, the more demonic they are as well. The bearers of the sciences now mobilizing themselves to combat chaos are not silly little professors, but there is a science more subtle than theirs. Demonism is a force. And to be forceful

means to overcome weakness, to *harm the weak.* Demon
is the master. The master will dodge any difficulty. And
will remain master. . . ."

When Scriabin finally discovered Helena Blavatsky and
read her *The Key to Theosophy* in 1905 (later he would
dip into her five-volume magnum opus, *The Secret Doctrine*), he found his wildest imaginings ratified. He modified his ideas somewhat, and incorporated some of the
Theosophical vocabulary—"plane," "astral body," "manvantara," "race" and "cycle." He already knew that sounds
had colors, but now he added to his palette Theosophy's
colors for vowel sounds and emotions—red for anger, yellow for intellect, grey-green for deceit, black for hatred, etc.
All this was according to Theosophy, and Scriabin concurred where he had not already affirmed for himself.
There are many cycles in time and in space, and the
divine play (this came from the Gnostics and the Stoics),
like the Brahman itself, never ends. Manvantara—the time
span of existence as we reckon it, beginning in the Original
Chaos and ending with the collapse of the solar system—
succeeds manvantara. OM is the mystic syllable Brahma
the Creator "saw," after being created by Brahman the
Supreme Being, and thinking how he might find the "ear
of the Ear, the mind of the Mind, the speech of the
Speech, the breath of the Breath, the eye of the Eye . . .
the utmost, the most adorable, most valuable, the inner,
final essence of all Essences." OM follows OM in unending succession.

Scriabin agreed up to this point. He felt the cosmic
process, the psychic process of cosmic will and feeling had
to be completed. He formulated his own "Rule," borrow-
ing the Theosophical word with its particular connotation:

0   Nothingness—Bliss
1   I wish. I rise out of Original Chaos, the Primordial Ooze

2 I differentiate the undifferentiable
3 I differentiate. I begin to define the elements of time and
   space, the future of the universe
4 I reach the summit, and from there recognize that all is
   one
0 Bliss—Nothingness

To Scriabin, the universe can achieve only one cycle.
The ultimate ecstasy or final unity cannot be repeated. His
mission was to marry life to eternity and thereby destroy it.
There could be no new wheel of life to turn. Brahman
must vanish within itself.

To a great extent, in being apocalyptic, Scriabin is simply a man of his times absorbing the pollen of ideas already in the air. Everyone was talking of doomsday. Every
Russian expected the end, "unheard of events and changes."
Eschatology was rife. And philosopher Vladimir Solovyov
had promised the nearness of "the end of human history."
(To Soviet rationalists, he predicted the atom bomb.) All
the symbolists wrote poetry apotheosizing world catastrophe. Dmitri Merezhkovsky, an acquaintance of Scriabin
and one of the most powerful men of Russian letters (another one of those "revolutionaries" under Tsardom and
"implacably hostile" to the Revolution under Lenin), had
made a sensation with his poem "Children of Darkness,"
epitomizing Russian thinking before the outburst of World
War I:

> We are on the edge of the abyss,
> Children of darkness awaiting the sun,
> We see the light, and like shadows,
> We die in its rays.

On the one hand, there was Scriabin's inherent affirmation of life, his dramatic heroics, "to do battle and love,"

as he wrote in his notebook. On the other, there was Blavatsky, profoundly influenced by Buddhism, asceticism, and committed to the removal of desire, including the desire to live. Scriabin resolved the opposing pulls of reason by placing himself in the center of the polarity. He had always wanted his music to create "physical shocks of sound power." Now, he wanted universal dissolution in Ecstasy redefined as Nothingness.

Originally, the "Mysterium" was to end in the destruction of the universe, a world conflagration (of which World War I was a prelude), literally international as the poets and playwrights had "sensed." Solovyov in his imaginative verse, pointed his finger, as we now read it, at the holocausts of war. One enigma remains: Out of this atmosphere around Scriabin of apocalyptic nightmares, sprang his radiant music. He sang, Danilevich points out, not of death but of life. Still, in one letter, Scriabin reminds a friend that "in this world, even death is beautiful." He loved life so much that he was willing to destroy it, but only to make it better and more beautiful . . . transformed by the beauty of *his* music.

As 1914 turned into 1915, Scriabin was less sure of the actual finale to the "Prefatory Action" or "Mysterium," according to Schloezer. They were to be the history of the universe—"the cosmo- and anthropo-genesis of the human race." Outwardly this would not be a recitation of historical events, but an inward story, the "forming" or "clothing" of the soul as it descended and submerged itself in matter and corporeality. The "Prefatory Action" as spectacle and performance presented the development of the cosmos, the emergence of all mankind, and the individual growth of individual personalities: from Oneness to Duality, into Multiplicity and finally to return to the initial Oneness.

The audience would experience this totally, psychologically and spiritually. In completed form the "Prefatory Action" would take seven days, and at the end of the twelfth hour of the seventh day, a new race of men would be born. According to Theosophy, we are the fifth race of men, so presumably the final extinction would come with the composing of the "Mysterium." Each day's performance would elevate the audience and performers to a new plane or level of sensation and vibration.

Schloezer states that Scriabin, at first, saw himself as the supreme high priest at the altar of this universal temple. (It was to be a half circle in India, with a pool of reflecting water to complete the full circle.) In 1915, he began to forget his own role and became dissolved in it, just as the ordinary spectator would. "I cannot do it alone," he said, "I must have assistance, so that people will understand the 'Mysterium' is a living act for all, all mankind, universal in concept, and not just a fancy in my head." Finally, he decided the end of the "Prefatory Action" would be defined in the moment of its very accomplishment. Men would become brothers, and brothers would return in some fashion to the Father. There would be a simulacrum of death, quite possibly like the facsimile of the ego's death under the influence of LSD.

On the seventh day, after the assault on the senses of all the arts battering at man's psyche, and with the music incarnating ectoplasmic visions, all men and all nature would combine to bring the world to its closest possible point of being on "the plane of unity." Mass joy would be like the ocean endlessly shifting and unchanging. Soul and matter would be released from their corporeal bondage one to the other. Male and female polarization would vanish. The divine androgyny of two sexes in one (as Plato once envisaged them) would first return and then become a nullity. Everything—man and his world—would plummet into the "ecstatic abyss of sunshine." The time lag between the event and the impact of the event would telescope.

At this final instant, the one Father flashes simultaneously into the consciousness of every auditor or spectator. Everyone then experiences an "involuntary Sonhood" of a sacrificial and martyrical nature. Yet the Father would not "be," because man would still be there conscious, experiencing, and in numbers. Scriabin would lead people to the threshold of death, the inexpressible, the unutterable. He would take mankind in a loving return to the Father, the birth of the Father, to a blessed immersion in Him, its resurrection, His loving receiving of his Sons, and our present manvantara would be concluded. "The act will then be crowned," Scriabin said. Then the ultimate act would be the forthcoming "Mysterium." All earth and earthly feelings would scorch in Scriabin's flaming soul. Man would be stripped of fleshly clothes. Matter would dematerialize in toto, and return to its purely naked, spiritual state . . . invisible and nonexistent.

"You rocks of my anger, you tender lines of my caresses, you soft colors of my dreams, you stars are lightning flashes of my glance, you sun, are my beatitude expressed in space. All is my temporal feelings. Thus I speak to you, bound by time and captured in space," he wrote in one notebook. He also wrote portentously, "The deed of Prometheus, the word of Christ, I am come to give you the secret of life and death." Whatever his means of reaching it, his personal ecstasy was so great that he was able to write, "My joy is so vast that myriads of universes could sink into it without even rippling the surface." With enticements as extravagant as these, little wonder that Scriabin in his lifetime attracted devotees, and at one time considered establishing a "colony" where he would teach ecstasy and demonstrate through his music.

Today, after all these dreams—some distressingly grandiose, others poetically hyperbolic, and still others, perhaps, even effective—what is left? The testimony of Scriabin's music. Beyond the words now in the far distance, the music still vibrates. It retains its magic, and conceivably comes close to achieving in us today what he aimed for then. He designed his music to be seen as well as heard, for it was to him "an orgy of visions . . . an astral world of emotions." He likened himself to the sun which asks nothing and which gives light, heat and life. He concerned himself with pure light and pure energy, and he tried to capture them in sound.

"Listen with your eyes," say the Buddhists. Perhaps Scriabin after all bizarrely arrested normal processes by some freak of nature, and did "walk in the sky," as Tibetans define the word "ecstasy." Maybe too, his music is an approximation, however imperfect, of nirvana or disintegration, taking us with it in an unbelievable victory of sound over our compulsive rationality.

Friedrich Schlegel, the German philosopher, once predicted that "Statues will become pictures, pictures will turn into verses, and verses become music and—who knows?" he added, "—perhaps someday great church music will take shape in the air and become itself a cathedral." If ever a composer tried to remove the veil separating possibilities from their probability, it was Scriabin. He permanently refused to believe in this world, which does not believe but only believes in believing.

VII   Creative Process

"I write in strict style," Scriabin used to say in the last years of his life. He did, although the music from his late period, Op. 58 on, sounds to the ear improvisatory, form-less, self-indulgent even. As late as July, 1972, Donal Hena-han writing in the *New York Times* described Scriabin, a man who never withdrew his allegiance to the sonata form, as "rambling and formally loose."

"There's nothing by accident . . . I compose according to definite principle," Scriabin said frequently, always pro-nouncing the word (which is the same in both Russian and English) as if it were spelled "prunciple." He used it to mean "system," a word which he did not use. And he would refer to a "secret harmony" in this piece or that. To the eye, the rigid structures of Scriabin's form looked clear, while the brightly painted chords with their honeyed har-monies, caroming modulations, and exfoliations of reso-nance remained mysterious and inexplicable. To grasp their organization it was almost as if, "You should be under the piano and look up," as Stravinsky said, later in his own late, serialistic compositions.

128

Just as *Prometheus* in 1914 had impressed the London audience by its philosophy more than its music, so too did the seductive, tonal atmospheres obscure their chordal, melodic and modulatory scheme, method, formula . . . "prunciple." Freedom cannot draw straight lines without firm design, Scriabin believed. Even during his lifetime, critics such as Mikhail Ivanov-Boretsky of *New Time* sensed Scriabin's strictness by calling him "a man of reason and illumination." But musical theorists, try as they might, from Scriabin's time to ours have diligently searched his structural and constructionist motives, only to find their analyses bladeless knives with handles missing.

Alexander Goldenveizer tells a significant anecdote in his memoirs. He writes, "Scriabin always said that everything in his later compositions was strictly according to 'law.' He said that he could prove this fact. However, everything seemed to conspire against his giving a demonstration. One day he invited Taneyev and me to his apartment so he could explain his theories of composition. We arrived and he dilly-dallied for a long time. Finally, he said he had a headache and would explain it all another day. That 'another day' never came. Scriabin was obviously afraid of Taneyev's destructive criticism."

Nevertheless, Scriabin was obsessed with wanting to convince Taneyev of his "melodic system and the laws behind the last period of his works," Dernova notes. "For everyone else [meaning the sychophants in the circle around Scriabin] he preferred to speak in terms of emotion and descriptive effects or impressions."

Taneyev had taught young Scriabin "strict style," meaning canon imitation, inversion, retrograde inversion, augmentation, diminution, and contrary motion, all in classical counterpoint. These theories, then, were applicable only to melody and those coinciding melodies which accidentally produced harmony. Obviously Taneyev, beaten with more and more sticks as Scriabin's music evolved into ever greater abstruseness, had begun "a venomous derision" of his former pupil, according to Goldenveizer whose own loyalty to Scriabin has already been mentioned.

Had Scriabin not had a "headache" that day, it is still far from certain that he would have been able to explicate his system to Taneyev and Goldenveizer. Like any creative artist, he had arrived at his system half intuitively and half through conscious awareness. He always worked from instinct, using logic after the fact to reinforce inspiration. One assumes the procedure of method stimulated his processes. As had Baudelaire before him, he struggled to capture "the drunkenness of the heart" while simultaneously demanding "mathematically exact metaphors." He insisted on combining "genius and lucidity," a rare but inescapable achievement in art. Civilization is the bringing of order out of chaos, and Scriabin wanted in his music to resolve the random world of pan- or omni-tonality into harmonious symmetry. He wanted music to be "like a sphere enclosing its center," and to prevent what a fifth-century Roman philosopher feared, "Music has lost the mode of gravity and virtue, and has almost fallen to baseness."

For sixty years now, musicologists have explored the geometry of Scriabin's architectonic schemes. They have found suggestions of the so-called *"Promethean"* chord in measures 26 and 58 of Waltz Op. 1, and in a mazurka or two from Op. 3. Still a riddle remained unsolved, unamenable to any consistent interpretation. With each attempt to understand Scriabin's harmonic system, it appeared as if yet another misapprehension was substituted for an old one.

Charles Rosen has spoken of the need to understand in order to listen: "The unity of a work of art is the oldest critical dogma that we have, and every piece of music de-

mands a perception of its unity in the absolute sense that
that is precisely what listening to it means. That is, the
unity is neither an attribute of the work, nor a subjective
impression of the listener. It is a condition of understanding: the work reveals its significance to those who listen as
if even its discontinuities correspond to hold it together."
But how to listen to the unknown, unfathomable Scriabin
harmonies, let alone understand them?

In 1968, the publishing house of Muzyka in Leningrad
issued *Garmoniya Skryabina* (*Scriabin's Harmony*) by
Varvara Pavlovna Dernova. For the first time, Scriabin's
code of chordal and melodic construction was broken. In
a detailed text (which unfortunately is impenetrably dense
in style, though not in concept) supported by a hundred
examples from various Scriabin compositions, Dernova defi-
nitively analyzes the system which Scriabin created and practiced. The reverberations from her discovery and revelations
are only now beginning to be graphed.

At this point, let us anticipate and say in simplified
terms that Scriabin's system consists of tritone links in enharmonic sequences which, in turn, produce whole-tone
and whole-tone-half-tone scales. A dominant seventh chord

with a lowered fifth (V_{b5}^7) or augmented fourth ($V_{\sharp4}^7$)

consists of two interlocked tritones (the tritone being three
whole tones, C to F♯ or G♭, for instance). Using this, Scriabin established a pantheon of what formerly were thought of
as dominant sevenths, ninths and eleventh chords, and exploited a series of alterations of their fifth notes—augmented, diminished and doubly augmented. These chords
take on an independent, self-sustaining life as tonal centers with their own implied or expressed simultaneous
"tonics," again to use inapplicable nomenclature for this
new concept of tonal stability. The tritone link and its

permutations form likewise the basis of Scriabin's "modulations," although this is again a misnomer, since the "dominance" of the harmony remains fixed and stationary. No longer can Scriabin's harmonies be understood in terms of "passing notes, suspensions, cambiatas or fermatas."*

If this knowledge were fully sensed in Scriabin's lifetime —perhaps, if the Scriabin-Taneyev-Goldenveizer meeting had eventuated—then Boris Schwarz's speculation would have come true: "Had it not been for the premature death of Scriabin in 1915, Moscow might have become a citadel of atonality, side by side with Vienna."

Miss Dernova was the brilliant pupil of Professor Yuri Tyulin, dean of Soviet musicologists at the Leningrad Conservatory, and she now is a leading professor at the Alma-Ata Conservatory in Kazakhstan. Unfortunately, her discoveries waited twenty years before acceptance for publication. To Soviet musicians, exposing the mechanical techniques of their most poetic and inspirational composer seemed rather like telling tales out of school. In Russia, where so many progressive, avant-garde movements once originated (think of Gabo, Malevich, or Kandinsky in painting and sculpture, Vakhtangov in theater, Mayakovsky, Akhmatova or the acmeists and futurists in poetry), rationalizations in art have been regarded with suspicion, as they were in America until recently.† Romantic nineteenth-century no-

* As Dernova wrote, "Alas, Scriabin's harmony is looked upon as some kind of corruption of classical harmony. This is a grave error. Scriabin had an inquisitive ear and an *intellect* in the highest sense of that word! It is not for us to 'correct' him, but for us to *study* him. We must take up arms against those who see Dual Modality as simply a double scale with tonic, dominant and subdominant simply twice duplicated."

† It would have been impossible for Pierre Boulez's statements to be printed or widely read, either there or here. This one, for instance: "I consider that methodological investigation and the search for a coherent system are an indispensable basis for all creation. Far from seeing the

tions of creativity still suffuse the esthetic experience in Russian minds. And this is why, probably, Dernova's exegesis was so long in coming before the world.*

Dernova presents her case forthrightly: "Scriabin's harmonic system is a unique phenomenon in the history of Russian music at the beginning of the twentieth century. All his creative work in the last years of his life was determined by one, very strict, thought-out, and unusually logical system. To it he subjected both his harmonic timbres and his sequences of harmony and melody. Using this system as a base, he erected his most precise and perfect constructions in the ideal. It was a very severe system and tolerated no deviation. Obviously, the composer found inexhaustible depths in it. In his last opuses almost none of his harmonies is ever repeated. Nor does he 'use up' or wear out those harmonies already found in the *Poem of Ecstasy* and *Prometheus* which so perplexed his contemporaries. He continued to disclose ever new and newer possibilities contained within the system."

She continues: "Did the system hinder the creative freedom of the composer, the life and poetry of his work? It is self-evident that this system was an obligation, a law and a discipline to which the composer subordinated himself. And this is testimony to the extraordinary development of its composer's intellect and gave him not abstractions but a living creativity full of colors and capable of the most

---

pursuit of a method and the establishment of a system as proof of a withering of the faculties, I see it on the contrary, as containing the most powerful form of invention, wherein the imagination plays an essential, determining role."

* It is interesting to note that in 1972 musicologist Ellon Carpenter at Kent State University, by studying Scriabin melodies, arrived substantially where Dernova had arrived examining the harmonies. Carpenter's thesis is titled "Thematic Development and Continuity in the Ten Piano Sonatas of Alexander Scriabin."

delicate emotional expressiveness. Not for the *sake* of the system did Scriabin work."

Dernova adduces at this point the "thoughtful, serious" and certainly "prescient" words of Prince Sergei Trubetskoi, Professor of Philosophy at Moscow University who reviewed that famous first all-Scriabin orchestral concert in 1902: "Scriabin's complexity is not artificial or made-up. It does not mask an absence of content. Rather, it is a consequence of musical thought trying to form itself, to express a truly complicated substance. Scriabin acknowledges no judge except the adjudication of his own personal, artistic conscience. He does not concede to the demands of the public. Rather, he makes on the public new, highly complicated and exalted demands of his own."

It was always said in Scriabin's lifetime that he was "not just a creator of art, but a creator of harmony." Now, after Dernova's revelation of his grammatical lexicon of music, what had once been "unconsciously sensed" surfaces openly into the "consciously known."

Victor Delson places Dernova's researches in his own context: "Scriabin in his later years, for all the genius of his intuition, began to give much more of his time and strength to constructing edifices of different proportions and symmetries, first counting out the number of measures in a work, the Seventh and Eighth Sonatas, for examples. Not by any means were any 'accidental' occurrences permitted in this composer's creative process. . . ." Delson pursues his point and rather launders Scriabin: "The Sixth and Eighth Sonatas are not without traces of intellectual schematicism and fabrication. But structural powers of genius appear even in these compositions. Here, inspiration aided by mastery often interrupts his plan. Living art surpasses all dogma. Doctrine is vacated, when confronted by the breath of true creativity."

Scriabin arrived at his harmonic revolution by many means, and via diverse paths. He worked simultaneously in a number of concrete and intangible areas. He had invented inside himself an astral world. Now, how to actuate it on the outside? His friend the electrical engineer Alexander Mozer, introduced Scriabin to Einstein's theories, physics, and quantum mechanics—sciences which Scriabin felt he needed to complete his intellectual grasp of the world. When Mozer explained the overtone series to him, he was intrigued by their letter-name similarity to the notes of some of his chords, and he figured that the stronger he could sound the upper partials, reinforce them that is, the more brilliant their "light" would become. Of course, on the piano this is impossible to accomplish. But Scriabin's legerdemain came close.

In Scriabin's sketches for the "Prefatory Action," there is one chord written out experimentally under the caption "Investigation: Melody, Harmony, Rhythm": C, F♯, B♭, E, A, D, G, and over it is written the overtone numbers, eight through fourteen (the twelfth, G, included). And on another page, he wrote out all the notes of the chromatic scale distributed musically for space, light and air.

For many years it has been erroneously asserted that Scriabin built his chord clusters on the basis of the overtone series, but he had already arrived at complicated harmonies, independent of Mozer's instruction. Sabaneeff spread this word and stated that the so-called Mystic chord (C, F♯, B♭, E, A, D) was based on an arrangement of the eighth, ninth, tenth, eleventh, thirteenth and fourteenth partials (the twelfth, G, being omitted). He further explained Scriabin's "ultra-chromaticism" on the basis of overtones, saying that the chords also derived from the eleventh to the seventeenth partials—F♯, G, A, B♭, B, C, D♭.

Scriabin's harmonic system was not based on overtones,

nor do they explain the direction of his harmonic development. Still, the misconception perpetuated. Ars. Avraamov in 1915 discarded the usual well-tempered adjustment of the piano and tuned it "naturally," so as to play the two Poems Op. 69 (written in 1913). He reported that ordinary tuning sounded "more consonant" than the artificially devised so-called "natural" one.

Conductor Nikolai Golovanov in 1918 had his orchestra—at least the strings and trombones—play their instruments according to just intonation rather than equal temperament. Anfilov, author of a popular book, *Physics and Music*, described these performances of Scriabin as "splendid." A. Eaglefield Hull, an early enthusiast and first Scriabin biographer in English, wrote in 1915, "Whereas Scriabin founds his chords on the pure temperament, his music is played and heard through the equal tuning . . . Nature herself accepts most of the compromises of the equal temperament, at any rate so far as the law of sympathetic vibration goes."

There were also experiments in performing Scriabin's music purely and pristinely with female voices and bells accompanied by string instruments with their natural intonation in an effort to escape the straitjacket of the twelve-tone piano octave.

Another tenacious misunderstanding was that Scriabin based his harmony on fourths and employed a quartal system of chord construction. Scriabin arranged some of his chord's notes occasionally in something approximating fourths rather than the traditional thirds, but he did not build his system this way. When he was once asked about the distribution of his tones in the opening chord of *Prometheus*—the questioner assumed it to be in fourths—he answered that the idea came to him in the simplest possible fashion, "I wanted to rid myself of the usual disposi-

tion in thirds of the dominant thirteenth chord." This
remark shows that in 1909 he was thinking in terms of traditional harmonic analysis. He also spoke of "the polarity of
tonic and dominant in *Prometheus*, but "it's at another
stage . . . on another plane." He was already applying his
system.*

For special timbre, Scriabin sometimes arranged, say,
what is reducible to analysis as a dominant minor ninth
chord with a diminished fifth (or augmented fourth) as
well as a perfect fifth ($V^{\flat 9\ 5}_{\sharp 4\ (\flat 5)}$) above the root of the chord,
as three augmented fourths or diminished fifths, tritones.
He separated the lower tritones by a perfect fifth, and the
upper tritones by a minor third or its inversion, a major
sixth.

In such a way he reached, for instance, the chord in
measure two of the Prelude Op. 74 No. 1 (written in 1914).

---

* There are, of course, roulades of fourths in the Eighth Sonata, and the
interval of the fourth is prominent in the central "I am" theme and its
expansion in *Prometheus*.

Such constructions or distributions may give the appearance of quartal harmony. However much as this and similar chords look like fourths (or diminished fifths) they are still triadic derived with alterations. "The pitches retain their tonal identity with tertian harmony," as Ellon Carpenter puts it.

A cursory glance at Scriabin's melodies shows how rarely he voiced them quartally (except occasionally in his "subdominant (IV) period," the Fourth Sonata, say, and later in the thematic exceptions of the Fifth). Overall, he even avoids his beloved tritone in melodies while being preoccupied obsessively with it in his bass harmonies. Ellon Carpenter, again, says: "The most common interval melodically, other than major and minor seconds which are unavoidable in pre-twelve-tone and pre-atonal music, is the third, major and minor, and its inversion the sixth, usually minor. This use of thirds reinforces the idea that Scriabin's concept of harmony was still basically tertian, not quartal. For if he had employed the fourth consciously as a harmonic interval, it would have shown up in his melodies too. . . ." The fact that fourths do not pull to the center, like thirds, still does not explain Scriabin's static, stationary poise devoid of resolution.

By trying to keep Scriabin's harmonies within the confines of the past and conventionally interpreting them on the basis of traditional analyses, some forced marches, stretches of the imagination, and mechanical reckonings have had to be made. Hull counted Scriabin's basic harmony as a "dominant thirteenth chord with a flattened fifth and a major ninth and the eleventh omitted." This sounds a little like the law which states: "If the facts do not fit the theory, then change the facts."

In examining the third measure of the Sixth Sonata, Howard Hanson calls it an "isometric tetrad" containing two major thirds, two major seconds, and two tritones. Even Pavchinsky has to reach far afield, when describing the opening of the Sixth Sonata. He places the "melody" in the tonality of Db Major and the harmony in D Minor. Again in the Albumleaf Op. 58, Pavchinsky places its melody in G♯ and the bass in the key of F♯.

Paul Dickenmann, the Swiss author of *Die Entwicklung der Harmonik bei A. Skrjabin*, describes one chord as a dominant ninth with the ninth in the bass, claiming that in the music from the Poem Op. 59 No. 1 onward, "In each measure there is a new chord, a ninth in the majority of instances. These consonances are no longer linked to one another functionally but present themselves unrelatedly, one after another as pure colors."

Scriabin cannot be analyzed by schoolbook harmonic rules which apply to another time and another world. Even those few people tumbling to his "secret" spitefully referred to his "bookkeeper's ledger of harmonic accounts." And it is amazing how doggedly people have clung to theories about Scriabin's harmonies despite evidence to the contrary. By confining Scriabin to the overtone or quartal theory, it is as if one looks at an oak tree and finds only one leaf . . . an elm, from another species.

The clue to Scriabin's harmonic system existed, at least in adumbrative form, during Scriabin's lifetime. Apart from Scriabin's own incomplete awareness, one man, Bole-

slav Yavorsky, foreshadowed our present comprehension.
Yavorsky was one of the most distinguished theorists of
modern times. He was a contemporary of Scriabin's, but venerated the music without subscribing to the shrine erected
around the person. By 1913 or 14, he had worked out the
basic principle behind all of Scriabin's chords and scales,
expanding it later into his now broad concept of Modal
Rhythm (*ladovy ritm*), using the word "rhythm" in a tonal
sense, the notion of unstable tones moving toward fixed
ones, as we will see in the next chapter. Dernova takes
Modal Rhythm as her point of departure for the road
which leads to her solving the baffling constellations and
configurations of Scriabin's music.

Yavorsky's friends urged him to meet with Scriabin and
show him his discoveries personally. Had he done so, Dernova's present-day conclusions doubtless would have been
reached during the composer's lifetime, instead of a half-
century later. However, Yavorsky, a "scientist" and "positivist," abhorred the hothouse, orchidaceous atmosphere
around Scriabin. He detested, not without reason, the
inner sanctum of "Theosophical fantasists," presided over by
Tatyana. He declined any introduction; so the two men
never met privately, or even at parties in their later
years. Scriabin heard about Yavorsky's theories and analyses
though, but the matter ended there.

On 16 April, 1915, the day after Scriabin's death, Yavorsky lectured about him at the Beethoven Studio in Moscow.
This was a major speech, outlining his ideas and placing
Scriabin in a perspective that no one had quite grasped
with such penetration before. The talk—later the basis for
his first published article—concluded by saying rather emotionally that, "Scriabin's lot in life was to be young. His
youth gave his work content and definition. It allowed him
to communicate, and so, pulls our hearts straight to him.
Yet it was also the reason for his untimely death. Had he

begun working sooner, he would have, no doubt, died earlier. He had to remain young."

Yavorsky divided Scriabin's total oeuvre into two periods, with the second period having three stages. The first period covers his first twenty opuses. These Yavorsky found typical of most composers belonging to the epoch of "psychological" nineteenth-century Romantic music. The music is marked by a sweetness, gentleness and unrestrained rubato; and "instability" of tonality begins to show precedence over "stability"; a prevalence of the fourth degree of the diatonic scale and its "subdominant" chords (IV) over the stronger, more pivotal "dominant" (V) or fifth of the tonality. From time to time, the subdominant mode establishes itself as equal in importance to that of the dominant. Only at the end is it overwhelmed by the dominant. Scriabin's Second Sonata is a case in point. There, Scriabin sustains the subdominant harmony, suspending it without resolution over long passages of many measures.

The emphasis on the subdominant was more than a mere emotional means for "expressiveness." It might be noted that Scriabin arranged his twenty-four Preludes Op. 11 (1888–1896) in a cycle of fifths (C-G-D, etc.) interleafed with their relative minor keys (A-E-B, etc.). His more advanced twelve études Op. 8 (1894–5), fell more than less in a cycle of perfect fourths (C♯ Major, F♯ Minor, B Minor, etc. and B-E-A Major, etc.).

The second period of Scriabin's work begins with the end of his "physical youth" at the age of thirty. Yavorsky divides all the subsequent music into three stages. Beginning in 1903, say, there is a clear upsurge in Scriabin's "social life," and his Op. 30's–40's music is characterized by intense nervousness and excitement. In the Fourth Sonata, Poems Op. 32, *Satanic Poem*, the *Divine Poem*, soft lyricism becomes "agitated and wearying . . . spasmodic." The dominant (V) chords based on the fifth tone of the scale overtake the subdominant (IV) and produce a "tension without relief." Scriabin "thirsts for activity," here, but "the parch cannot be slaked," Yavorsky stated. He finds no "active resolution, no release into stability." However, this tension stimulates "a further splurge of energy."

In Scriabin's larger compositions among the Op. 30's and 40's, he uses C Major as his "chief tonality," although in lesser pieces he shows a leaning to F♯ Minor as an adjacent tonality (situated a tritone away from C).

Everywhere in Scriabin's early works, he seems to be struggling out of the minor key into the major, as if already searching for inter-modality. The first movement of the First Sonata ends by going from F Minor to F Major, the end of the second movement goes from C Minor to C Major. The last measure of the sonata almost abdicates by leaving out the major or minor third in the empty chords of open fifths. Passages of the Third Sonata waver precariously between F♯ Major and F♯ Minor, as if Scriabin simply cannot make up his mind.

The early posthumous Fantasy for Piano and Orchestra proceeds from A Minor to A Major. In the late Prelude Op. 74 No. 2, listen to the F♯ Major key section vacillating between brackets of F♯ Minor, or to the simultaneity of A Major and A Minor in No. 4, particularly contrasting the opening chord of A C-C♯ E. Here the note, minor C, is in the treble; whereas in the final chord, again A C-C♯ E, the major tone, C♯, is on top as if opening out into a triumphant emphasis.

The Soviets juggle points looking for emphatic sunniness in those early works in major keys and tonalities. To Westerners, Russian music is apt to conjure pictures of mournful minor keys. These belong more to Russian gypsy music, and are not typical of "Russian" music as a body, exemplified by Glinka and his sparkle, wit, and brightness.

Several Soviet theoreticians have done theses on the major or diatonic aspect of Scriabin's early work. V. Berkov wrote, "A serious analysis of Scriabin's harmony reveals its national character, golden threads which tie it to Russian folk song, as for example in his use of major keys." And L. Koposova cites Scriabin's "attachment to major keys and Russianism, particularly in pieces such as Etude Op. 8 No. 5 in E Major, Prelude Op. 11 No. 15 in D♭ Major, Prelude Op. 16 No. 3 in G♭ Major, and the theme and variations in F♯ Major in the second movement of his otherwise minor Concerto.

And even Yavorsky himself considers the sad Prelude Op. 74 No. 2 as being in F♯ Major although clearly to the ear it is in minor, if either mode must be accepted. Ellon Carpenter suggests that Yavorsky may have counted the A♯ which is heard in thirteen of the thirty-four quarter-note beats; whereas the A natural is heard only six times. Further, the A natural is always in the uppermost voice, and the A♯ in the lowest treble voice. But this, again, is an instance of Russian ears hearing differently from ours.

As for the minor keys, the Prelude Op. 51 No. 2—marked to be played "lugubriously"—(1906) was Scriabin's last piece "incontestably" in the minor mode, and it sounds, amid all his rapidly progressing and advanced work of that period, like a curious throwback, a reversion to some distant melancholy, possibly an earlier sketch he only sent to the publisher because he needed quick money. Scriabin, indeed, refused ever to play this piece, and excused himself by saying "it will break the piano strings." More and more as Scriabin grew older, he disliked any minor cast to music. It contradicted the light and radiance he was looking for. It impaired the positive aspects of his psychological working out away from tragedy.

Gradually, as well, Scriabin's thinking turns against the

major mode, a fact all the more extraordinary coming as
it does after his abolition of minor keys. His tonality in
major keys begins to "decompose," as Yavorsky puts it.
Inter-modality sets the pattern.

In the second stage of the second period, Yavorsky cites
Ecstasy Op. 54 (replete with long delayed resolutions to C
Major) and other pieces from the Op. 50's. Here, Yavorsky
says, Scriabin has unearthed an "entire storehouse of modes
and means" to "establish" even greater tonal "instability."
The dominant seventh (V^7) chord supersedes all else.
Because of the tritone created by the added seventh, it
becomes an "irritation" or "tension without exit." Scriabin
now avoids any relaxation into "resolution" or even cadences—those "most muscular of intonations," as Asafiev
says. Hence the beginning of ambiguity in Scriabin's chords
during the Op. 50's, a state of affairs which lasted until his
system was fully formulated.

The third stage of the second period, according to Yavorsky, commences with *Prometheus*. With the condensation
into one-movement structures, Yavorsky asseverates what
he calls "inactive maintenance," an indication of "physical
fatigue." Everything seems to suggest a "languid" feeling
of weariness, he says. But there is still "the illusion of
earlier youthful tensions, strains, and efforts." He places
the Ninth and Tenth Sonatas in this category.

Now, and it will remain so to the end, the logic of
tonality and its scales becomes uniformly united. "All orna-
mentation stems from the initiatory, cellular consonance,"
the tension of whose dominant chords is its most important tool.

Yavorsky compares this period in Scriabin's creativity
with the Ninth Symphony of Beethoven, Rimsky-Korsakov's opera *Kitezh*, and the last period of Liszt, and notes
there in those men a similar "waning . . . a decline and

fall," as he puts it, but not in the pejorative sense these words contain. Yavorsky never missed a Scriabin recital in his lifetime and passionately adored and pored over the late works. But he believed that all genius—like the sun living off its own energy—burns itself out and exhausts its own fuel. He called the Prelude Op. 74 No. 2 "The soul of Scriabin's swan song . . . the last, damp trace on sand from an exhausted, vanishing, dying wave." And for this reason, Scriabin would have died sooner if he had begun composing earlier. As he said, "He had to remain young."

VIII   Harmonic System

Scriabin exited from the halls of classical harmony by rejecting the idea of "absolute tonal stability," by generating
chords outside the major-minor context. He treated his
complicated, altered and embellished dominant (V) chords
as consonances asking no resolution, moving only from one
into yet another unstable dominant concord.

By recognizing various nuclear dominants at the core of
all Scriabin's most advanced music, we understand how
Scriabin was more of a culminating point than an innovator in himself. He was not, for all his originality, "a tailless
comet," as the Russians say. For this reason, too, Scriabin's would-be epigones had little success in following along
his blazed trails. As Prokofiev would later admonish his students, "Above all, no ninth chords, please!"

While Scriabin was probably the first composer of the
twentieth-century to emancipate tonal relationships within
scales and chords and to "invent" a new composing formula, he nevertheless maintained ties with traditional triadic
harmony, as he had earlier maintained ties with Russianism. His system was completely new and purely Scriabin
. . . a climactic end to exhausted possibilities.

146

It was also a total entity within itself. "Melody is harmony unfurled," he often said and would add, "Harmony is furled melody." In this way, he leveled the vertical and horizontal differences between harmony and melody to a single unit of compression. Melody lost definition, surrendered its legibility as a line separate from harmony's integer. After being a supreme rhapsodist in his early days (the "songs" of the B♭ Minor Etude Op. 8 No. 11, the slow movement of the Third Sonata, etc.), Scriabin's melodies turned motivic, fragmentary parts of the whole of the music's tonality. As Briussov put it poetically, "Scriabin wanted to melt the metal of melody and mold it in new form."

Late Scriabin, thus, often sounds like Anton Webern, just as middle Scriabin, in the Fourth Sonata, reminds listeners of George Gershwin. John McCabe hears Ravel in the Fifth Sonata, although in all of these instances people are indeed putting carts before horses.

Scriabin reinforced his new tonal centers of gravity by the repetitive use of the tritone. The tritone divides the octave into two equal halves, as opposed to the fifth and fourth division of the octave in its tonic-dominant relationship. The tritone inherently became indispensable within his altered, added-to, constantly modified dominants, treated now as "new" tonics and tonalities.

Scriabin made less than might be expected of enharmonic spellings. His orthography does not explain. The piano, of course, cannot differentiate in sound between say an F♯ and a G♭. The Second Sonata was originally written in A♭ Minor, although it appears in its printed edition in the key of G♯ Minor. Belaieff, in this instance, must have pointed out to him that A♭ Minor has as its related major C♭, a key which does not exist for any practical purpose, even if the Harvard Dictionary of Music does include it in its Circle of Fifths. Often, when we compare a Scriabin manuscript with its published version, we find discrepancies in the musical notation. Evidently, Scriabin had no firm theory about the difference between a diminished fifth and an augmented fourth. It would appear that he sometimes felt differently when he sent a manuscript off in one form and saw it returned in galley proofs. He had afterthoughts, but what they were we cannot decipher.

The Fifth Sonata Op. 53 (1907), the last sonata in which Scriabin used a key designation, F♯, was drafted in its first version with six flats, G♭, as its signature. Subjectively speaking, the "feel" of this sonata is perhaps more that of flats than sharps, although Scriabin by and large associated sharps with an upward movement, the sense of rising life and flight (the *Presto con allegrezza* main section, for example). Logically, sharps might indicate, too, greater luminosity, although the *estatico con luminosità* coda in both versions bears the signature of E♭.

In this same piece, a characteristic, six-tone Scriabin chord—a dominant ninth chord with both a raised and a lowered fifth ($V_{\flat 5}^{\substack{9 \\ \sharp 5}}$) sounded simultaneously—appears veiled by its orthography. The crystal second theme of the introduction marked *languido* (symbolizing "distant dreams, languor, enchantments," as Scriabin said, "emotionally" to intimate friends), presents the chord in B Major—the dominant being F♯, A♯, C (lowered fifth), C𝄪 (raised fifth), E, G♯—in its third inversion on the note E. In measures seven and eight of the *languido* section, C𝄪 is written as D, and C natural as B♯. The *Meno Vivo* section is in B♭ with the emphasis on its dominant F. In measure seven here C♯ (raised fifth of the dominant) is written as D♭ and C𝄪 as D.

After Scriabin dispenses with key signatures altogether, beginning with the Poem and Prelude Op. 59 (1910), his enharmonic logic becomes less arbitrary, although at times the accidentals continued to change during their transition from manuscript to print form. The Poem-Nocturne Op. 61, for instance, has a preliminary draft which shows a majority of its notes written with sharps as accidentals. The published version gives the same equivalent notes with flats. Obviously, Scriabin's system was in constant flux, formulating itself ever more clearly in his mind, if not perceptible to us.

Bykov, the Soviet musicologist, observes that there is a paradox between Scriabin's indifference or changeability regarding enharmonic spellings of the same tone, and the binding, specific precision and logical clarity of form he used in his outlines. His manuscripts contain rows of empty measures with only a designation as to their tonality or supporting harmonies. He specified so many blank measures simply by count or number, to be filled in later with music. A framework was vital to Scriabin. It conveyed, Bykov thinks, "the subtlety of vibrations" he heard within "his microworld of harmony, melody and rhythm."

As said earlier, the tritone is the crux of Scriabin's harmonic system. Composers such as Paul Hindemith thought that music without the interval of the perfect fifth was static, passive, and suffered from a loss of tension (Debussy's, for example). Hindemith did not understand, let alone like Scriabin. However, in Scriabin's music the tritone was clearly the most essential ingredient used and he exploited it. Acoustically, perhaps it did not have the functional validity of the traditional basis of chord movement. Intellectually, it posited perfectly a system *not* dependent on the release of tension yet containing within itself all the necessary tension. As Delson points out, the minor third leads to the diatonic scale; the tritone leads to Dual Modality, as defined by Yavorsky.

Scriabin delved into ancient music of Greece, as part of the self-education he underwent in the last years of his life. However, he could not have known what we now know, that the Pythagorean basis of our tuning rose not from Greece of the sixth century B.C. but from Sumeria, via Babylon, more than 3,000 years ago in Mesopotamia, giving it even greater antiquity.

Scriabin was cognizant, though, of the basis for deriving the modes used in ancient music. If the musician took a harp, say, and played the scale in a succession of perfect fourths, in each scale he strikes one tritone. For example, starting from C (–F, D–G, E–A, etc.) the tritone appears at F. To ancient ears, and to more modern ones for a long time, this was a disharmony, a bedevilling interval which needed rectification. So, the musician changed this tritone to a perfect fourth (F,–B♭). Then starting his second scale with F, including the first adjusted note, B♭, (F–B♭, G–C, A–D, etc.) he arrived at the tritone B♭–E which he changes to E♭. Repeating the process seven times, creating seven modes, he returned to the original scale of C a quarter-tone (or less) in place of the expected perfect unison. This last, of course, would be out of tune to our ears, accustomed as we are to equal instead of natural temperament, just as the upper partials of the overtone series are "sharp" and "flat" to our corrupted ears.

Thus, the Pythagorean tuning we recognized as the origin of our own scale, and whose pitches were in use until around 1500 A.D., while it worked better than the original "just intonation," could not meet requirements for enharmonic tones at a keyboard instrument. It was eventually replaced by the equal temperament we accept today.

Scriabin, almost perversely, took this rejected tritone, and because of its "naturalness" to the hand on the keyboard, its logical symmetry (order out of chaos, again) and its voluptuous sonority, consciously made it fundamental to all his harmonic distributions. It therefore lies at the foundation of Yavorsky's analysis. The linking of tritones provides the mechanical sound source for his variously elaborated conceptions.

As a result of exploring new ways of looking at harmony, Yavorsky was forced to invent a new language (Modal Rhythm, for example). He also designated the particular basis of Scriabin's harmony, Dual Modality (*dvazhdy lady*), a system for forming various scales derived from tritones and linked by tritones into resolution (either inward into a major third, or outward to a minor sixth). Dual Modality combines pairs of tritones to create a kind of bitonality in each given piece of Scriabin's music.

First Yavorsky took the tritone as unstable (represented in the examples by black notes) requiring resolution into a major third as its stable or tonic interval (open notes). He linked these in a chain, separating them at a distance of a minor third, the symmetrical division of the tritone in half.

Then he linked the tritones and their resolution at the intervallic distance of a major third.

To form what he called a "Double-Augmented Scale" he linked two successions of tritones resolving into major thirds. The second chain starts with an inversion of the bass tritone, B–F (or E♯), which becomes E♯–B.

5

The stable and unstable tones each form a separate whole-tone scale which is in itself composed of three linked tritones. Russian composers since Glinka have used the whole-tone scale (long before Debussy) to express "supernatural" and "fairy tale" incidents. And, similarly, Rimsky-Korsakov anticipated part of Scriabin's system by treating the diminished seventh chord as a consonance, a stable tonic, in *Kashchei*.

6

Yavorsky then links a shorter succession of tritones and their resolutions at a distance of a minor third (as he began in Example 3), again starting the second series at the distance of an inversion of the initial tritone (B–F).

7

Thus he derived the "major-minor" scale, or what he called the "Double-Step Scale" (formed from the stable, or open, notes). This we know by the cumbersome designation, "Alternating Half-tone and Whole-tone Scale," one of those "gypsy" modes Scriabin discussed with Casals in 1910, having already arrived at it.

8

This was the scale which Scriabin used in the Sixth Sonata (1911) which was the first of his sonatas to be built entirely on his new system.* It can also be found in certain pieces of Chopin and Liszt, and in Glinka's opera *Ruslan* and in Rimsky-Korsakov's late works. Dernova, synthesizing Yavorsky's Dual Modality system, combined the unstable tones in Example 4 to arrive at the Scriabin hallmark, a dominant seventh chord with lowered fifth (V_{b5}^{7}), also classifiable as the French Sixth, or two major thirds separated by a major second. In other words, enharmonically, two interlocking tritones.

Dernova writes: "Only after examining the strict, logical, and polished system opened up by Scriabin in his enharmonic spellings of the dominant seventh chords with lowered fifths, can one discuss those Scriabin harmonies

* "Enigma" Op. 52 No. 2, composed in 1907, was the first piece entirely built from Scriabin's new system, although there had been earlier works such as the Etude Op. 42 No. 2 (1903) composed "wholly according to mathematical formula." In the miniature "Enigma," for the first time he turns his back completely on resolutions into tonics (in his bigger works, for a while, he will continue to resolve conventionally, if often belatedly), and it was for good reason that he called it—at Tatyana's suggestion—"enigmatic." He himself was puzzled by its harmonic structure of chords linked in a tritonal chain. The piece also uses the Enharmonic Sequence, which explains his exiting into C despite the key signature of Db and use of the dominant (V) chord on Ab as a stable "tonic."

"Enigma," further, was the first composition, aside from poems or dances, to which Scriabin gave an unusual title. He began to make all markings in French ("Enigma" is marked *"étrange, capricieusement"*), as he had first begun, tentatively, in the *Divine Poem*. No longer would he use the Italian affectations he resorted to in the Fifth Sonata, *accarezzevole, presto tumultuoso esaltato*, etc.

which startled his contemporaries so much. It would be incredible to suppose that these harmonies with all their never-repeated individuality could have arisen independently of his whole structure of musical thinking. Therefore, any research into those extraordinary harmonies of the last period—the '*Promethean*' chord, the harmonies of the Sixth and Eighth Sonatas, preludes and poems of the last opuses—must return to the dominant chords with lowered fifths, from which origin he started constructing his modal system. As we have already said many times, the chief and fundamental function of the dominant chord with lowered fifth is to form the Tritone Link which is the basis of Dual Modality. Forming the Tritone Link of altered dominant chords gives the complexity to the dominants formed from the Tritone Link."

First, Dernova establishes the enharmonic equality of such a chord (V_{b5}^7), which she writes in Russian fashion as D_7^{-5}, in this case G, B, Db, F, belonging to the tonality of C, and respelled (as Scriabin often does) as Abb, Cb Db, F. In this guise the same chord is the second inversion ($\frac{4}{3}$ chord) of the dominant seventh (with a lowered 5th) belonging not to C but to Gb, a key which is also a tritone's distance from the rightful tonic of C. Here, clearly, is Yavorsky's Dual Modality—the same chord belonging to two tonalities simultaneously.

9

In Scriabin, the unification of these two tonalities (C and G♭) separated by a tritone is not only an evident means of modulation. It forms a Tritone Link, which produces two separate, autonomous chords. Dernova designates the first as Departure Dominant (*Da*), since it assumes an initiatory significance in Scriabin's music. The second she calls Derived Dominant (*Db*). *Da* and *Db* are like a brother and sister having related but equal and independent function within a nuclear family of harmony.

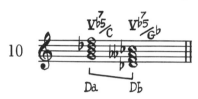

10

As did Scriabin, Dernova goes on to add one more of the unstable notes (the sixth will be added later) as shown in (Yavorsky's) Example 5. The Departure Dominant (*Da*) thus develops as a major ninth chord with a lowered fifth (V_{b5}^{9}). When this is respelled enharmonically as a second inversion, it yields a Derived Dominant (*Db*) whose tonic is again a tritone distant from the Departure Dominants. With the addition of the ninth to the *Da*, the *Db* becomes a dominant seventh in root position with a jointly lowered and raised fifth ($V_{b5}^{7\#5}$). Yavorsky called these dominant chords with expanded and contracted fifths, "split fifths," in a convenient economy of words.

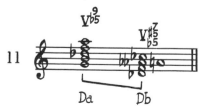

11

The Departure Dominant (*Da*) in an added guise as a minor ninth with lowered fifth (V_{b5}^{b9}),* when respelled enharmonically and linked at the distance of a tritone to produce its Derived Dominant (*Db*), now becomes a dominant seventh with both a lowered and a perfect fifth (V_{b5}^{7}).

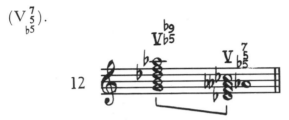

Note that the raised fifth of Derived Dominant (*Db*) is the major ninth of Departure Dominant (*Da*) in Example 11, while the perfect fifth of Derived Dominant (*Db*) in Example 12 is the minor ninth of Departure Dominant (*Da*). The root tone (G) of both Departure Dominants (*Da*'s) in either example, major or minor ninths, stays the diminished fifth in both Derived Dominants (*Db*'s). This, according to Dernova, demonstrates the mutual interdependence of tones in the Tritone Link.

Resulting from this interdependency within the Tritone Link, by respelling the chords, rethinking them as Departure Dominants (*Da*'s) and Derived Dominants (*Db*'s), and adding the sixth note from (Yavorsky's) Example 5, Dernova arrives at six different possibilities: two dominant seventh chords with lowered fifths (V_{b5}^{7}), as in Example 10; two dominant major ninths with lowered and raised fifths (V_{b5}^{9}), as in Example 13; and two dominant minor ninths with lowered and perfect fifths (V_{b5}^{b9}), as in Example

* Yavorsky described this chord, the V_{b5}^{b9}, not only Scriabin's, but Chopin's and Liszt's "calling card." They left it everywhere they went.

14. (Example 14 is derived from Example 13 by alteration
—major ninth to minor ninth.)

Taking each note of the first dominant major ninth
chord in Example 13 with its lowered and raised fifths
$\left(V^{\sharp 9}_{\substack{\sharp 5 \\ \flat 5}}\right)$ in scalar succession: A, B, D♭, E♭(D♯), F, we find
six dominant major ninth chords each with a lowered and
raised fifth. These chords all have the same notes as
sounded on the piano, but each has its own internal significance. Each contains within itself the whole-tone scale and
three interlocking tritones. (Here Scriabin anticipates Josef
Hauer, the spiritual author and "practitioner" of twelve-
tone music, and his theory of tropes.)

15

These are the most characteristic of Scriabin's so-called
"six-tone" or "synthetic" harmonies. When they are arranged to form what Dernova calls the "Enharmonic Se-

quence" or "Major Enharmonic Sequence," as in Example 16, the Enharmonic Sequence of six equal dominant chords or Departure Dominants (*Da*'s) and Derived Dominants (*Db*'s) forms three basic Tritone Links, the fourth link repeating the first. The Sequence begins and ends with the starting Departure Dominant (*Da*). The Departure Dominants (*Da*'s) form the whole-tone scale ascending and descending. The Derived Dominants (*Db*'s) connect with the succeeding Departure Dominants (*Da*'s) at the intervallic distance either down a major third (two whole tones apart instead of one) or its inversion, up a minor sixth.*

16

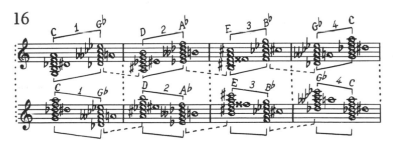

According to Dual Modality, each of these dominants may be understood to have a tonic, but it is a tonic that does not appear. "It is heard only in the imagination, from a far-off perspective," Dernova writes. The tonics cannot be heard, because of the complexity of the dominants. Scriabin actually sounds them, often at the end of some of his advanced pieces. The effect is surprising—very tender and gentle—and the added fifth below melts into the unstable concord of tension, but scarcely serves as a resolution.

When the basic Departure Dominant (*Da*) or G, say, is respelled at the tritone D♭ to form its Derived Dominant (*Db*), the raised fifth becomes a major ninth interval

* Rachmaninov has an instance of this sequence in his Etude-Tableau in E♭ Minor Op. 39 No. 5, written in 1917.

above the root of the *Da* chord. Therefore, the whole-tone relationship between the D♭ and the D♯, the raised and lowered fifths of the chord at the tritonal level, in the *Db* chord, becomes a major ninth apart instead of the major second (in the original *Da* chord) or minor seventh , when (in the succeeding *Da* chord) the chord is transposed down a major third, or again a minor seventh when transposed up a major third. This is Scriabin's preferred distribution (or displacement) of tones within such a chord.

The diminished and augmented fifth tones regulate the movement of the dominant major ninth chord to the major third below or minor sixth above, and define the two enharmonic respellings at the tritone and at the interval of a major third. The control, as musicologist Roy Guenther of Catholic University in Washington, D.C., points out, exerted by the relation and movement of the diminished fifths (tritones) and augmented fifths replaces the gravitation of roots a fifth apart in tradition.

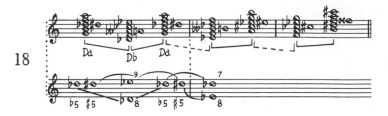

In other words, because of the originating effect of the Departure Dominant (*Da*) in Scriabin, it often appears as if first forming a three-way tritone link: Departure Dominant (*Da*)-Derived Dominant (*Db*)-Departure Dominant (*Da*). It is not necessary to repeat *Da* to accomplish the modulation by enharmonic spelling. This can also be done between *Db* and the following *Da* (a whole step). Taking the pairs of chords in sequence, the next chord following the initial tritone link is a *Db*, not a *Da*. The *Da*'s are separated by whole-steps, as are the *Db*'s. *Da* must be repeated in order to continue the chain or sequence—*Db*–*Da*; *Db*–*Da*, etc. A modulation from *Db* on D♭ to *Da* on E♭ can be accomplished in this way. It is not exclusive between the two *Da*'s. This enharmonic succession of up a tritone down a major third is only possible with a major ninth chord (with lowered and raised fifths) which yields the whole-tone scale. The entire sequence of Example 18 is nothing more than a constant regrouping of the same six tones or pitches.

When Scriabin's chords contain seven notes, they are usually duplications of tones, so as to arrive at the special timbre and transparency (or cloudiness) he wanted to signify for his own specific reasons. He cannot add a note without disrupting the whole-tone tonality of the above-mentioned Departure Dominants (*Da*'s). The Dominant minor ninth chord (with alterations) cannot be arranged according to the whole-tone sequence.

Scriabin continues to complexify. As in Example 12, if you take the Departure Dominant (*Da*) as a dominant minor ninth chord with lowered fifth, and respell it enharmonically at the distance of a tritone, you reach the Derived Dominant (*Db*) of a dominant seventh chord with a joint lowered fifth and a perfect fifth.

Now, starting from a Departure Dominant (*Da*) that is a dominant major ninth chord with a lowered fifth and a perfect fifth, and respelling it at the distance of a tritone for its Derived Dominant (*Db*), which has a minor ninth and a raised and perfect fifth, and respelling it again at the pitch of a major third lower, as Dernova did with the major ninth chord in the whole-tone sequence, we arrive at the perfect eleventh chord with a raised fifth ($V^{11}_{\sharp 5}$).

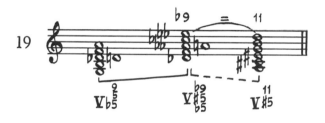

If you take the eleventh chord ($V^{11}_{\sharp 5}$) and lower or raise its eleventh note, D into D♭ or into D♯, you reach the basic Departure Dominant (*Da*) on G, but with an extra note. This sequence cannot be repeated, because the dominant major ninth with lowered fifth and perfect fifth ($V^{9}_{\flat 5}$) contains one tone which disrupts the whole tonality, the D which makes the perfect fifth. This D or perfect fifth creates the minor ninth chord in its enharmonic inversion at the distance of a tritone above, and the eleventh in its movement (respelling) down a major third. If you lower or raise this tone, to resolve it, it becomes either the third

of this dominant chord, the new Departure Dominant
(Da), or its diminished fifth.

Taking the E or perfect fifth of the dominant eleventh
chord (derived from the original Departure Dominant
[Da] which is the only note in the eleventh chord which
does *not* fit into the whole-tone scale, Scriabin returns to
the original Departure Dominant (Da) *with* this E. This
note now becomes a major sixth tone above the G or root of
the departure Dominant (Da), a further obscuring of the
regularly dominant-sounding chord.

In traditional harmonic analysis, it is the major thirteenth above the root. But Scriabin uses it in the lower octave with the fifth and seventh notes. This tone is as well
the major third of the tonic—another subliminal implica-
tion of Dual Modality. (E, for example, taking C as the
tonic when G is the root of the dominant chord.)

The explanation for this tone is difficult. It is a third
variant in Scriabin's arsenal of altered dominant seventh
and ninth chords—a branching out, a trifurcation or double augmentation of that flexible, magical fifth tone. The
first two variants are of course the dominant seventh or
ninth chord with the raised and lowered fifth ($V^{(9)\,7}_{\#5\,\flat5}$), and
the dominant seventh or ninth chord with the perfect and
lowered fifth ($V^{(9)\,7}_{5\,\flat5}$).

This "accessory" or added sixth note has particular and
very great significance for Scriabin. Dernova gives it the

letter "V" when it belongs to Departure Dominant (Da), and "W" when it appears in Derived Dominant (Db). It requires a special designation since it is vital to Scriabin's system.

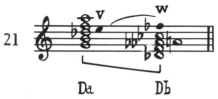

"V," and "W" especially, weaken the potential pull of the dominant harmony into any resolution. "V" differentiates its Departure Dominant (Da) from all others. In the enharmonic sequence of transpositions and inversions, just as the perfect fifth becomes a minor ninth, the raised fifth a major ninth, the sixth changes into the minor third above the root tone of the Derived Dominant (Db). (It is, incidentally, a minor third below the root tone of the Departure Dominant [Da] and can be regarded as the symmetrical division of the tritone in half, as the tritone itself halves the octave.)

"V" in the Departure Dominant (Da) sounds traditional for reasons already noted, but in the Derived Dominant (Db), as "W," as a minor third, it clashes with the overriding, strong major third. (The "V" is E in Example 22, with the "W" being Fb.) The simple resolution is to retranspose by respelling the Departure Dominant (Da) tritonally where the tension between the seventh (F) and it (E) as a sixth is weaker.

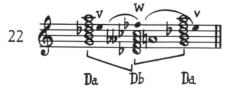

Other reliefs from the "W" in Derived Dominant (*Db*) tension exist. Melodically, for instance, "W" can move a half-tone higher to become the third of the Derived Dominant (*Db*).

Or it can go a half-tone lower to find repose as the major ninth of the Derived Dominant (*Db*).

To recapitulate, as we see from their enharmonic possibilities, a "legality" issues from the dominant chords with lowered fifth. This interval makes possible Tritone Links, which in turn create two enharmonic equalities. The enharmonic equalities may be regarded as equal dominants separated by a tritone, Departure Dominant (*Da*) or Derived Dominant (*Db*), or they may be regarded as two "fused" tonalities. Remember that from the Tritone Link, the Enharmonic Sequence (up a tritone down a major third to form a progression by whole tones) becomes possible. But in these examples, what takes place is no more than a respelling of tones of the dominant sevenths and dominant ninths with, of course, a corresponding alteration of "meaning" or inherent tonality within each structure.

Scriabin in his music—an example of practice over theory —prefers to handle these nuclear chords of his system as "supplementary" to one another. By omitting the lowered fifth from the Departure Dominant (*Da*) he opens a window on the sonority and allows the alteration to appear as the root of the Derivative Dominant (*Db*). Thus, two dominant sevenths are required before the chord reaches its sum total. (There is a case for two "understood" tonics here, again, which provides a further potential for complexity.)

In Scriabin's harmony created by the Tritone Link, he moves from the root tone of the first dominant seventh chord to the root tone of the second dominant seventh chord, keeping all the tones of the first dominant in place. This is what Avraamov in his article, "Ultrachromaticism or Omnitonality," published in *Sirius* (Petrograd, 1916), called felicitously (and Dernova accepts the phrase), the "composite bass." From it, he said, all of Scriabin's "complicated harmonic complexes" rise. All the tones of the sonorities envelop themselves around this.

To supplement or complete dominant major ninths with the conjunctive lowered and raised fifths, Scriabin employs the enharmonic sequence. Continuing this sequence to six links adds nothing new, since we already arrive at the inversion of the Departure Dominant (*Da*) beginning with the third Tritone Link. The link only repeats itself.

26

Any harmony that disrupts the whole-tone tonality must be arrived at by other means. The minor ninth chord with lowered fifth and perfect fifth, for example, consists of two major triads (dominant sevenths lacking their sevenths), separated by a tritone, the "*Petrushka* Chord."

27

The dominant major ninth with raised or lowered fifths, which is an arrangement of the whole-tone scale as we saw earlier, is the basis of all Scriabin melodies, once his "singing melodies" of the earlier period disappear from his rapidly fragmenting music. There is no separate melody in Scriabin, as such, but only "harmonic melody" and "melodic harmony," as Dernova puts it.

28

Here is how the system operates in even as early a piece as the "Poem of Languor" Op. 52 No. 3 (composed on

8 June, 1905). This is one of Scriabin's erotic pieces, "languor" sometimes having a specifically sexual connotation in his mind.

29

The existence of Departure Dominants (*Da's*) and Derived Dominants (*Db's*) presupposes their tonics, as said earlier, which Dernova designates as *Ta* and *Tb*. Here she shows the tonal relationships within the dominant major ninth with lowered and raised fifth ($V_{\sharp5}^{9}$).

30

Now, she adds the "V" and "W" accessory tones to the integer.

31

Here, the related tonics *Ta* and *Tb* are shown.

32

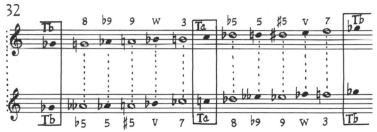

This in brief, simplified form is the basis of Scriabin's harmonic system, as presented by Dernova.

The question is not whether Dernova has invented a system as complicated as Scriabin's own heretofore inexplicable methods—there is no alternative explanation, despite the critical cries of her opponents. Forcing his harmonies into conventional theory analysis creates really inapplicable superstructures. Dernova has unlocked the door which, as we see, opens onto a room not only of infinite variety but of unexampled—up to that period of time—intricacies, elaborations and continuing fertilities.

Examination of Scriabin's compositions substantiate Dernova's findings. Here is how the Albumleaf Op. 58 looks in her schematic outline, with both *Da* and *Db* having their tonics, *Ta* and *Tb*, sounded. Note that the piece consists of twenty-three measures, technically, sixteen measures in harmonic analysis, and approximately twelve pedal measures, counted by Scriabin's own markings. In general, Scriabin has marked the pedal to be held for every two measures—a remarkable study in sonority blurs, and a clear indication of how he heard his group of harmonies as single consistencies.

33

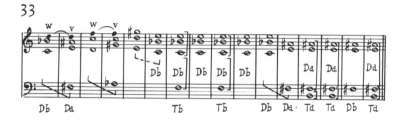

The mystery of the much-debated "Promethean" or "Mystic" chord now appears neither as overtones nor as quartal harmony, but only as one among the many dominant chords Scriabin used widely and variously as *Da*'s and *Db*'s. Strictly adhering to his remarkable system, with its specific additives and subtractions, he based the chord and redistributed its spacing by inverting its seventh with its root. He did this for the "obscure, misty" effect that he wanted. Before the piece was widely known, he would play the chord and then defy anyone to pick it out by ear, so

sure he was of his disguising his method's origins and their
inherent tonal values. This highlights what Danilevich pro-
claims as the most important factor in Scriabin, the fact
that you cannot define his harmony on the basis of what it
sounds like. The tonality of this chord is A, and Scriabin
saw the color green (as he marked the score of *Prometheus*)
when it sounded.

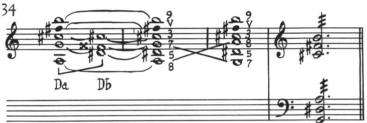

A further highpoint of Scriabin's harmonic complexity
is to be found in the following examples. Here, "V" and
"W" take on, as said earlier, vital significance. They develop an independent character integral to the music itself,
permitting the formulation of more and more complex
chords. The Prelude Op. 59 No. 2 (1910) marked by Scriabin "savage and bellicose," as Dernova has analyzed it:

The beginning of the *Allegro* in the Eighth Sonata Op.
66 (1912), again in Dernova's analysis of Scriabin's most
baffling composition:

36

Ellon Carpenter points out that "Not until Schoenberg with his twelve-tone technique do we find a composer so consistent in his compositional technique . . . and Scriabin comes so close to this 12-note system that it seems probable he would have taken it as the next logical step."

In any event, Schoenberg only made his venture in that direction the year of Scriabin's death. And Scriabin, even as it was, might easily have been constrained to point out —in another context, of course—as Schoenberg was once forced to write, "My works are twelve-tone *compositions*; not *twelve-tone* compositions." So, too, paralleling this, Scriabin wrote "systemic *music*."

IX   Ten Sonatas

The world has been lavish in its praise of Scriabin's ten sonatas. Even those persons most reluctant to accord him any high seat of honor in music history nonetheless pay respect to this body of his work. Certainly, in every sense and from any number of points of view, the sonatas are extraordinary as *oeuvre* with Scriabin as *auteur*.

The ten sonatas have afforded scholars a near-inexhaustible source of analysis and approach. Their harmonic continuity one from the other, their slow break with the past of traditional music, their elaborate and elaborative programmatic content, their meaning (aside from the conflicting interpretations Scriabin himself gave them, according to his entourage of followers), and their abundance of rhythmic invention and complexity are unparalleled.

Scriabin may have studied other people's orchestration, Rimsky-Korsakov, Glazunov, Debussy, Strauss, but the sonata as he saw it was entirely his own concept. Steadily, over the course of twenty-one composing years from 1892 when he wrote the First Sonata to 1913 when he finished the Eighth Sonata, from the age of twenty to forty-one, he made the sonata central to his corpus of creativity, developing it according to his uniquely personal ideas.

What is there to compare with these sonatas for piano solo? Debussy's Preludes and Etudes, perhaps. Ravel's *Miroirs* or *Gaspard de la Nuit?* Berg, Busoni, Ives, Rachmaninov? Elliott Carter's Sonata? (It was Scriabin's music which determined Carter to become a musician, as confessed in his *Flawed Words and Stubborn Sounds.*) Whatever one's personal taste may be, only a recalcitrant few contest the highwater mark, the honored position in all of twentieth-century music which the Scriabin sonatas occupy.

As a Russian, Scriabin lacked traditional models. The sonata form has always been conspicuously absent from Russian music. Balakirev, Tchaikovsky, Glazunov and Liapunov made lonely excursions in the direction, but Scriabin was the first Russian to use the sonata as a basic platform for continuous expression and to achieve genuine masterworks from and through it. Of course later, there were Medtner's fourteen, highly uneven and heavily worked sonatas, and Prokofiev's rivalling masterpieces. Frederick Martens, thus, can say unequivocally, "With Scriabin, both as regards to quality and quantity, the Russian pianoforte sonata may be said to begin." In Russia itself, Asafiev, doyen of critics, expressed a consensus when he wrote that Scriabin's ten sonatas are "the highest point in the evolution of the Russian sonata."

More and more as we advance toward the twenty-first century and understand our own the twentieth better, we realize that Scriabin as culminator-innovator was the first to point many new musical directions. The most striking aspect of his sonatas is the progression—both as personal autobiography and as original music—they represent. In this, he resembles Beethoven. Almost seamlessly, they move step by step into greater and greater emotional complexity and musical technicality. Each, like those sculptured Grecian heads of antiquity, is slightly larger than life. Each tells more about the craft of music than we had before surmised.

The sonatas move without a break from conventionality into modernity, from nineteenth-century intensity and discursiveness into twentieth-century condensation and economy. Unlike Debussy with his abandonment of Massenet and exploitation of the Javanese whole-tone scale, or Schoenberg's casting off Wagner's spell and plunging into dodecaphony, Scriabin's decalogue of landmarks proceeds slowly. For a long time when the winds of "modern music" were being opposed as a discontinuity of history, these sonatas were studied as examples of how inevitably and logically music could advance from the past into the present and future, from consonance into dissonance.

Scriabin had some initial difficulty (perhaps because he had no indigenous tradition to support him) in composing sonatas. He made three youthful essay attempts while still a teenager at the Cadet Corps. At thirteen years of age, in 1885, he composed a little piece, more a sonata in name than in size, and its babyish music interests only the connoisseur. At fourteen, he wrote a Fantasy Sonata in G♯ Minor—an inflated nocturne, really—and its two movements surprise by their charm and skill. (This piece is not to be confused with the Second Sonata Op. 19, also a Fantasy Sonata in G♯ Minor and in two movements.) In 1887, he composed a Sonata in E♭ Minor whose first movement was published as the Allegro Appassionata Op. 4. As a whole, this last sonata astonishes by its keyboard command, much as its turgidity, perhaps, annoys.

Posthumous pieces of music, or early music suppressed from publication by the composer during his lifetime, are like stepchildren—there, but unwanted. Anna Akhmatova, the great Russian poet who heard Scriabin in one of his last recitals, has said that "Just as the future ripens in the past, so does the past decay in the future." Scriabin in each sonata allows the future to become itself by ridding itself of the very past which made it possible. Scriabin may not have allowed the publication of these works—and for good reason—but he nevertheless kept the manuscripts safely in his files, and one day even went over them carefully, dating them accurately while cocking half an eye at posterity.

Taking the ten sonatas as a body of work, one is quickly struck by their variation in form and shape. Two are vast in scope, in four movements—the First in F Minor Op. 6 and the Third in F♯ Minor Op. 23. Two are in two movements, a sort of slow introduction and rapid finale—the Second, and the Fourth in F♯ Major Op. 30. The remaining six are one-movement sonatas.

Throughout all ten sonatas Scriabin maintained his loyalty to the sonata form—what Edward Kaufman calls "his attachment to the sonata form"—although in the last six there are no longer any compulsory modulations. The tonic-dominant relationships in the exposition and recapitulation, and the modulatory separation of the first and second subjects attenuate themselves out of all conventional understanding or recognition. After the Fourth Sonata, cadences vanish; and with the Fifth, many familiar, visible elements of the sonata form disappear. Still, Ellon Carpenter points out that except for the Sixth, Op. 62, all the sonatas from the Fourth on "contain an opening prelude which then dissolves into the more vigorous sonata form." In general, the last six sonatas consist of an introduction, exposition, the development of two groups of themes, a recapitulation or réprise, and a vertiginous coda.

The First Sonata is motivic in that its four movements (unusually, all in the key of F Minor, except for the slow

second movement in C Minor) are linked by an ascension
of three notes, to put it most simply. This motif reoccurs
continuously, either as initiatory theme or simply as an
interruption to remind the listener at once of what he has
already heard or will hear in yet another form elsewhere.

This use of themes or motifs changes as Scriabin develops his independent ideas. Four of the sonatas have apotheoses. Themes heard in totally different context or in a
separate movement, recur as climaxes to make the composition self-identifying or self-identical. In the Third Sonata
the ringing, singing *andante* melody of the slow third
movement becomes, unexpectedly, the climactic *maestoso*
culmination of the last pages of the last, fourth movement.
After all the wandering and operatic hyperbole of the Third
Sonata, as a whole, Scriabin zeros in on this theme. Its
sweetness is transubstantiated into grandeur in the middle
of a fugato finale.

The gentle *andante* opening theme of the Fourth Sonata
expands maximally as the final climax of the second and
last movement. In programmatic terms, the "languor"
theme transforms itself into the "will" theme in the development and coda of the second movement. The languor
theme in the first movement ends with a descending minor
sixth (augmented fifth) marked by stress marks and the
notation *con voglia* (with will). It should be noted here
that languor, so characteristic of Scriabin's slow themes,
for once in this instance, carries no sexual connotation,
only that of desire or longing. It is this which the *con
voglia* marking emphasizes, as much as it suggests the
sublimation from passivity to highest activity to come.

Another *languido* theme, the first theme of the Fifth
Sonata, Op. 53, becomes apotheosized into the grandiose
estatico ending of this sonata. Similarly, although the
sense is different, the center theme of the Ninth Sonata

Op. 68, marked *"avec une langueur naissante,"* after being developed in the *"pur, limpide"* section turns into the grotesque *"alla marcia"* at the sonata's end.

Considering the variety of form within Scriabin's sonatas, it can be mentioned in passing that three of the sonatas are bracketed—the Fifth, Ninth and Tenth Op. 70—and end as they begin, repeating their introduction as final conclusion. In all three, this introduction appears midway to punctuate the end of the exposition section and heralds the development. In the Ninth and Tenth Sonatas the introduction is treated as a generative theme, integral to the composition, and undergoes a series of developments and permutations embroidering it in the texture of the whole piece.

Soviet musicologist V. Bobrovsky develops a theory of what he calls "musical dramaturgy." Taking Scriabin's famous dictum (already mentioned on page 55), "From the greatest delicacy (refinement) via active efficacy (flight) to the greatest grandiosity," he labels progression A, B, and C. This he finds to be the basic structure of all Scriabin's music.

The "highest delicacy" or A, is something "intangible but lofty." The light from a distant star which marks the opening of the Fourth Sonata, for instance. It also can be something pastoral, as in the opening of the Tenth Sonata, or it can be a mood or feeling, such as Scriabin's famous "languor," he says, sexual or passive.

B or "active efficacy" can be flight, as in the second movement of the Fourth Sonata, playful animation (*jeu divin*) as in the *Presto con alleggrezza* section of the Fifth Sonata, or fanfares—calls, summonings or invocations—as in the openings of the Sixth and Seventh Sonatas.

"Greatest grandiosity" or C, is Scriabin's life-affirming "I am." This takes a variety of forms in his codas—the transmogrifying apotheoses of the sonatas mentioned earlier, for instance—or in bursts of bell sounds which he invokes for key sections of the Sixth and Seventh Op. 64, the only "bell" sonatas, or even in a march as in the Ninth Sonata.

Characteristic of the later sonatas are vertiginous codas, ecstatic climaxes, and cosmic dances of atoms, in which everything disintegrates and blows away like dust into outer space. The Sixth, Seventh and Eighth Sonatas, for example, evaporate in a flutter of trills, as if the auditor is left grounded watching the spectacle of the music disappear in the distance above him.

In general as the sonatas progress, the music becomes more "decompositional" or "self-transforming," rather as a cigarette progresses by being consumed by fire from phosphorous to flame to embers to extinction and silence. Scriabin in his later music turned away from the use of music to express psychological or emotional states, and wanted to achieve what he called "dematerialization . . . incorporeality . . . disembodiment." It followed that those lovely melodies of his young years dissolved into kinds of spin-offs from other voices heard in other worlds. As the "building blocks" became smaller, "tighter governance" took over, Kaufman observes.

In content, two of the sonatas can be regarded as purely psychological, subjective expressions of Scriabin's soul states and personal feelings—the First and the Third. The First, as mentioned earlier, with its gloomy Funeral March, is a tragic cry against God for having permitted the hand injury of 1891. The Third is more sophisticated and for it Scriabin composed a "text." The Soul or Spirit passes through a series of vicissitudes—suffering, battle, pleasures, "a sea of feeling." In the midst of a tempest, the voice of the Man-God or Creator-Man rises. He shouts a song of victory, but still weak, He falls back into the abyss of nothingness. This was composed during the honeymoon of his disastrous first marriage.

Three of the ten sonatas may be considered nature pieces. The Second portrays the sea. In 1892, on a trip to Latvia, Muscovite Scriabin saw the Baltic Sea for the first time. He conceived the Second Sonata, and enlarged his conception the following year when he went to Yalta and was much moved by the glittering moonlight on the Black Sea. No piece of Scriabin's music ever caused him so much trouble or took so long in composing. He worked on it again in 1895 when he visited Genoa and saw yet another sea, the Mediterranean. In general, the sonata, remarkably short for the five years it took him to compose (he finished it in 1897), depicts the sea in its various phases of tranquil depth, storm and agitation.

Scriabin himself never attached a program to the Eighth Sonata, his longest and probably greatest among later works, but scholar Asafiev perhaps discloses the composer's extra-musical intention when he wrote, "On contemplating the Eighth, I associate it with the physical world and the laws of energy: light, darkness; heat and cold; the rhythms of night, waves of the ocean, its pulsations, its sighs, the feeling of fire and air."

The music is brilliant and dazzling, although the sections marked *tragique* have puzzled listeners and performers. Can it be that the sadness of man intrudes in this world of nature? The sound itself belies Scriabin's marking, even when taking into consideration that "tragic" in Russia means "heroic," rather than "pitiable."

The Tenth Sonata has been discussed earlier, and it, like the Fourth, concerns light specifically. Scriabin said to Goldenveizer and composer Nikolayev about the climax (the section marked *puissant, radieux*). "Here is blinding light as if the sun has come close. Here is the suffocation one feels in the moment of ecstasy. This was hinted at in the Fourth Sonata. There too is a kind of asphyxiation from radiance . . . winged flight . . . light." He uses trills incessantly for luminosity. Trills to Scriabin were "palpitation . . . trembling . . . the vibration in the atmosphere," and a source of light.

The Seventh Sonata was Scriabin's favorite. He spoke of its six-tone "secret harmony," meaning the Derived Dominant (*Db*) and Departure Dominant (*Da*), harmonies on which the piece builds. He called it "purest mysticism," and felt that in it he had at last achieved "the highest complexity within the highest simplicity," for finally his system was clear and concentrated, while the message it conveyed was ultimate and absolute. He nicknamed the sonata his "White Mass," and it constitutes his only sonata which can be classed as sacerdotal, saintly, or beatitudinous.

In the Seventh Sonata, Scriabin for the first time confronted absolute logic and made it into purely inspirational music. In this piece he expresses his philosophy in sound—the contrast, interplay and interrelation of the poles of subject and object, spirit and matter, male (active) and female (passive) principles. The Seventh Sonata is a purification, because it describes the process of opposite poles touching, merging and fusing. The world (object) is transformed by the artist-creator (subject) who leads us through ecstasy into dematerialization. In the course of this ideological journey, the Seventh produces, according to Scriabin, a variety of effects—chords of perfume, mystic bells of sanctification, fountains of spraying fires, vortexes of wind, a final dance of ecstasy. On one level, Scriabin shows us the magical effect on the world of the Will, or subjective spirit. On the second level, he shows us how the "other world" manifests itself in this plane through sound. By those concepts, Scriabin poses music insurmountable problems. One cannot hear saintliness in music as abstract concepts, any-more than one can hear, say, homosexuality in Saint-Säens or Ravel. Just as logic denies visible evidence, music, like language, has its own logic. It is this which Scriabin put to service for himself, and which variegates our hearing of his music.

Two of the ten sonatas represent, theologically, the Left-Handed Principle, as opposed to the Right-Handed Princi-ple, the Sixth and the Ninth. Although such concepts as evil, satanism, demonism are certainly as difficult to hear in music as any other morality, Scriabin considered these pieces to be nightmarish visions of wickedness. When he played the Ninth Sonata he said he was "practicing sor-cery." It is not surprising that the Sixth and Ninth were composed simultaneously with saintly and radiant counter-parts, the Seventh and Eighth, almost as if antidotes to each other. Scriabin played the Ninth often enough, but refused to perform the Sixth. Nor did he ever perform the First or the Eighth; and from his letters we can deduce that clearly he had pianistic difficulties with the Third and Tenth.

Mention should be made of the question of key designa-tions for the later sonatas. The Fifth is "legally" in F♯ Major. The Sixth Sonata, less legitimately, was originally titled as being in the key of G Major, but without key sig-nature. Publisher Koussevitzky felt the world of 1912 was not yet ready for such extremes of anchorless tonality. The student purchaser of sheet music, he reasoned, needed a hook on which to hang the greatcoat of his understanding.

When Scriabin authorized the key of G, he was supply-ing a tonal center. Actually, the Sixth is composed of G and D♭ together, the Departure Dominant (Da) and De-rived Dominant (Db), respectively. He did the opposite with the Seventh Sonata, when he performed it for the first time in public on 21 February, 1912, a year before the appearance of the piece in print. There the program listed its key as F♯ [The F♯ denotes the Derived Dominant (*Db*) and C, the Departure Dominant (*Da*).]

Sabaneeff assigned the key of the Eighth Sonata as "A." Jurgenson, following Koussevitzky's tradition, printed the first edition in A, and the Ninth and Tenth Sonatas as being, respectively, in G and F. Scriabin approved these designations as much to indicate color as to express the focus of their inner tonalities—G being "rosy orange," F "dark red," F♯ "blue," and A "green," according to his color scale.

X   Five Symphonies

Nothing like the respect shown the sonatas has been given to Scriabin's five symphonies. They were badly received in their day, by and large, and only now arrive at any appropriate recognition. They seem to have weathered the past's disapproval and ensuing neglect. In Soviet Russia, Scriabin is regarded as a master symphonist. After all, they ask, who else wrote symphonies between Tchaikovsky and Shostakovich? (Russia has been as short on symphonies as it was on sonatas.)

To us in the West, Scriabin's orchestration is more French than Russian. To Russians he is completely Russian, and they remark on his skillful use of the high registers of brass, the transparency of his woodwinds, and his rich, affectionate handling of the violin, particularly in solo passages. More recently, Westerners are finding Scriabin something better than a piano composer transcribing for orchestra. Conductor Robert Craft, for instance, cites the first movement of the *Divine Poem* (Third Symphony) for its "eerie luminosity" in the woodwind octave passage marked *mystérieux, romantique, légendaire*. The *più vivo* section shortly before this, Craft finds, "as suggestive of

183

the sensation of 'caressing' as any music this side of the 'Feelies.'"

Scriabin's oeuvre is divided, at least in music schools, into three connecting but separate periods: Early (up to the Fourth Sonata), Middle (including the *Divine Poem* and *Ecstasy*), and Late (beginning with *Prometheus*). But the music Scriabin composed during his years as professor at the Moscow Conservatory (1898 to 1903) is so apart that it constitutes a category all its own. How, for example, can one consider both the First and Second Symphonies as "Early"? And how can they be separated from their mates, the Preludes Op. 27 and the Fantasy?

It is too strong to dismiss this Conservatory music as derivative. But it is inspissated with the steam of academe, monuments to the culminative rather than innovative aspects of Scriabin's genius. The music is particularly correct, studied, structured and formal. To some, these pieces establish Scriabin as a bona fide musician with soundest of credentials. To others, this period of music is a frustrating delay of the real Scriabin to come.

The First Symphony in E Major Op. 26 is an enormous work in six (nearly seven) movements, requiring a grand orchestra, mezzo-soprano and tenor soloists, and a full chorus. Only the fourth movement, *vivace* in C Major, a miniature scherzo lasting about three minutes, was successful in its day. Conductors usually had to repeat it. Scriabin was crushed by the hostile reception given the symphony— boos, catcalls, and more insulting, whistles—although Safonov had called it "the new Bible." But he was sadder about his failure in the choral fugue which ends the symphony by apostrophizing art.

> Come, all peoples everywhere . . .
> Praise Art!
> Glorious forever!

Scriabin had wanted to establish his conviction of the transforming power of art over life in a poem, and to be as international and universal as possible, he composed a fugue to it. He would try again in the next symphony, this time choosing a march. He failed both times, and he knew it. But his goal remained a desire for the triumphant sublimation of suffering into joy.

The Second Symphony in C Minor Op. 29 is a masterpiece of turn-of-the-century music. Like the first, it is massive (but without singers) and in five movements, each in a different key and each with unusually contrasting rhythmic variation to differentiate between them. It is also vast in its loyalty to conventional classicisms—sonata-allegro form, rondo, even canonical imitation. For instance, the slow third movement *Andante* in B Major, is exceptional in that it contains a fully developed sonata-form instead of the more usual abbreviation of the exposition and recapitulation for middle movements in symphonies.

Delson calls the Second Symphony a "monothematic unity," since the first movement establishes the theme of the whole work (bars two and four, clarinet; compare four bars after Figure 11 in the second movement; one bar before Figure 80 in the fourth movement; and the main theme of the fifth movement). He likens it to a sonata-form enveloping a sonata-form, seeing the first movement as introduction; the second movement as the main statement of the exposition; the third movement as its contrasting statement; the fourth movement, where all the themes of other movements are recalled, comprises the development; and the fifth movement is a recapitulation, réprise and coda.

Delson associates the Second Symphony emotionally with a painting by Mikhail Vrubel of the same year, 1901. It tells of the Titanomachy, the defeat of Titan deities by Olympian gods. Although Vrubel, like Scriabin in this his

most tragic composition (except perhaps for the First Sonata), depicts loneliness and defeat, there is still titanic
strength, power, protest, nobility and struggle.

Scriabin labored hard over this symphony. He had particular difficulties with the second movement *Allegro* in E
Flat Major, as his sketchbooks show. The rhythmic changes
from $\frac{6}{8}$ to $\frac{3}{4}$, and the excellent melody were arrived at after
many versions, changes and experiments. The third move-
ment *Andante* with its bird calls and "loving pantheism,"
as Delson describes it, came more easily, perhaps because
"happiness and contentment with life," as Arnold Alshvang titles this movement, supplied quicker impetus for
Scriabin. Nature, as mentioned earlier, appears surprisingly
in Scriabin's music. He.used bird calls again in the Third
Symphony, this time to express "voluptuousness." But the
Andante of the Second Symphony is hardly "a veritable
aviary," as Nicholas Slonimsky called it.

Scriabin throughout his life was unusually critical (for
him) of the Second Symphony. The *Maestoso* finale particularly disappointed him. He had for the first time
wanted light in music, a radiant triumph of man over life's
obstacles and defeats. What he got was "a military pa-
rade." He blamed his failure on his striving for something so
simple that all people of the entire world might understand
— time and straight, diatonic triads* in the key of C Major. *Tut u menya ne vyshlo* ("Here I didn't bring it off"),
he often said to friends. And when Modest Altschuler
asked to perform the symphony in New York, Scriabin declined. "I liked it when I wrote it, but now it doesn't please
me anymore . . . the last part is banal." Scriabin planned

---

* For radiance in music Scriabin continued to revert to triadic chords,
viz. the Tenth Sonata.

to rewrite the ending, but by this time, his mind had moved on to other kinds of music.

Time has reversed these critical attitudes towards the Second Symphony. As musical personal history, it is matchless. In the context of Russian symphonism, it remains a seven-league stride forward, although Scriabin later chose not to follow its compositional direction.

Today in retrospect it is astounding to read Liadov's reaction to the Second Symphony. (Scriabin wrote it quickly from 19 January to September, 1901, and sent the manuscript off in pencil.) "What a symphony, but what kind?" Liadov scribbled disparagingly on the manuscript in a note to Belaieff. "After Scriabin, Wagner lisps sweetly like a suckling babe. I think I'll lose my mind. But where can one hide from such music? Help!"

After the first performance in St. Petersburg, conducted by none other than Liadov himself, on 12 January, 1902 (Vera had just given Scriabin her fourth and last child), Arensky wrote a nasty letter to Taneyev who wanted to know how the performance had gone. "In my opinion the program erred when it said Scriabin's '2nd Symphony.' It should have said '2nd Cacophony,' because this 'composition' lacks almost all consonance." The Second Symphony sounds remarkably tame as listened to by posterity.

In 1903, Scriabin liberated himself from the Conservatory, and from all of this kind of Conservatory music. His philosophical ideas were well on the march into their mystical, magical purlieus of the incredible. He composed the Third Symphony in C Minor Op. 43, and subtitled it the *Divine Poem*. For the first time he gave titles in French to the separate movements of the symphony and to make its meaning clear and international: *Luttes* (Struggles), *Voluptés* (Sensual Delights), and *Jeu Divin* (Divine Play). Scriabin appended a text to the *Divine Poem*, not a poem but program notes of explanation, compiled by Tatyana and Boris Schloezer in French. It describes the Ego divided into Man-God and Slave-Man. They struggle with each other, and proceeding through the total concord and discord of human experience, finally reach unity and that longed-for divine freedom which enables man to exist playfully as god himself in the sky of other worlds in blissful ecstasy.

The form of the *Divine Poem* incidentally is an exception to Bobrovsky's A-B-C theory. The piece begins with "self-affirmation," C, and ends with B, "flight" or "playfulness." Too, it may be noted that Debussy wrote his symphony *La Mer* in the same year Scriabin wrote the *Divine Poem*. There is small doubt that the former is the finer piece of music as a whole. But it might be remembered that Debussy was ten years older than Scriabin at the time and that, ultimately, he was not so advancing an innovator.

Scriabin normally composed rapidly (the Fifth Sonata in a week, each symphony only a short work-year), but some pieces seemed to take forever. In the same way that he had labored over the Second Sonata, the *Poem of Ecstasy* took almost three years, from 1905 through 1907. One reason for this, clearly, was the massive intellection that formulated in his mind simultaneously with the inception of the music.

At first he did not know that the composition would become his Fourth Symphony. He thought of it initially in terms of an orgiastic or orgasmic poem (*"Poème Orgiaque"*) in which Man-God arrives at release through love and sex, creation and procreation. The freedom of untrammeled action (as in the *Divine Poem* whose idea he borrowed from the Stoics of ancient Greece who spoke of their "divine, mindless play"), would suffuse the entire world, dissolving it into ecstasy. Meanwhile, as a matrix of order to hold the genius of his ideas and their sounds in music together, he composed a text in poetry.

Scriabin attached considerable importance to the poem of "the *Poem of Ecstasy*" The words as well as the music expressed his philosophical doctrine or "teaching." It is Spirit's great self-assertion, *Ya es'm* or "I am," reached after a gamut of emotions and experiences—delicious excitement followed by soothing languor, terror, doubt, "the maggot of satiety . . . the bite of hyenas . . . sting of serpent," intoxication, burning kisses, spiritual and temporal love-making and, ultimately, ecstasy.

Since music is self-sufficient and a world within itself, it is, of course, subject to countless interpretations. Scriabin at one point in 1906, under the influence of Georgi Plekhanov, described *Ecstasy* as "music reeking of Revolution . . . the ideals for which the Russian people are struggling." And it is incredible today to recall that during *Ecstasy's* Russian première in St. Petersburg on 19 January, 1909—the world première had taken place in New York on 10 December, 1908—composers Prokofiev and Miaskovsky sat side by side exchanging glances of bewilderment at not understanding a note of it. Some critics, however, spoke of its "enormous impact . . . brilliant scoring . . . the most daring composition in contemporary music."

And it is also astonishing to look at all the hundreds of sketches and drafts of the *Poem of Ecstasy* preserved at the Central Museum of Musical Culture in Moscow. The main theme—self-assertion intoned incessantly by trumpets—underwent countless transformations. The key keeps changing. The ascending skips change in interval and the theme's compass at first exceeds its octave range. Over one version Scriabin wrote a line which does not appear in the final text, "Why, whither are you striving, Oh rebellious Spirit?"

The *Poem of Ecstasy* as music sings one theme. Scriabin

once said to Ivan Lipaev, "When you listen to *Ecstasy* look straight into the eye of the Sun!" The brass—and the score requires eight horns in F, five trumpets in B♭, three trombones and tuba—timidly announces this theme of Self-affirmation, a short ascending melody in shrinking intervals —a fourth, major third, minor third—marked *avec une noble et douce majesté*. It continues through all the vicissitudes of doubt and terror described in the poem's text, until it triumphs over the total orchestral climax of all instruments at full blast. Its musical tension produces the resounding "I am," the orgiastic climax.

Its free sonata form consists of an exposition and development almost identically paralleling each other. The music is passively languorous and emaciated at times, dramatically fearful at others; twisting and turning, it strongly and unrelentingly builds and increases, slowing down only to speed. It softens so as to harden and passes through shudders of fleeting ravishment—*moderato avec délice* (with delight), *presque en délire* (almost deliriously), moments marked *charmé* (enchanted). *Ecstasy* continues unabated toward the beginning of an orgasm with the clarinet sweetly singing, and finishes in spirit *and* flesh. All color disappears here; only volume remains (the score calls for a pipe organ). Then a brief coda of weariness. The end sees the composition's resolution in C Major.

Scriabin's fifth, last and greatest symphony was *Prometheus: the Poem of Fire* Op. 60. A "symphony" because like *Ecstasy*, it follows the sonata form, and a "poem" because it is free, with the development and coda longer than the exposition and recapitulation.

Prometheus' composition, despite the gigantic scale of the expanded orchestra—solo piano, masses of trumpets and horns, special bells, organ, chorus and light effects—demanded only a swift year, 1909. Sabaneeff describes the composer's first mention of the piece. They are at a party at Koussevitzky's home in Moscow. Scriabin turns abruptly and says, "What plans I have, what plans! You know, I have lights in *Prometheus*. [He whispered the word "lights."] "I will play it for you. Lights. It's a poem of fire. Here the hall has changing colors. Now they glow; now they turn into tongues of flame. Listen how all this music is really fire."

Later he expatiated, "What dreams I sometimes dream. But they are not dreams, but visions, illusions which become tangible, sounds in pictures . . . That which will be . . . that which will be. You know, there are tempi so slow in *Prometheus* that no one has ever before played so slowly. Don't you think that music bewitches time and can stop its ticking? Eternity must stretch from the moment of languor to complete dematerialization . . ." And the conversation became lost in Scriabin's special vagaries.

This *Poem of Fire* was the first multi-media composition actually calling for light effects in the score. As early as 1891 in Paris the *Song of Solomon* had been performed as a "spiritual symphony" with sound, light and perfume. Soon after in America *A Trip to Japan in Sixteen Minutes* had been staged with geisha dancers, perfumes and music. But Scriabin lifted "shows" from commercialism and spectacle into serious art. In *Prometheus*, he wanted the tonalities made visible as they progressed. He wanted to center the eye in the ear's sonorities.

In the score, the top line of the *tastiera per luce* (a color instrument which at that time did not even exist, except in Scriabin's head and in Mozer's assurance that it could be made) denotes the tonality, and changes as each tonality changes. The bottom line is mystical, a progression in whole tones which represents the breathing in and breathing out of the Brahman, the evolution of the race by steps.

Scriabin, it must be pointed out, did not see colors as individual tones, but as tonalities and chordal complexes. Later he moved from color music into light music, from a visual dependency on the aural sounds into an independence between colored lights and composition.

He shared this feeling for optic music or chromophonia with Rimsky-Korsakov who had written well before the *Poem of Fire*: "Harmony is light and dark. Major and minor. Joy and sorrow. Clarity, shadow, duskiness. Orchestration and timbre in general: sparks, radiance, transparence, shadings; brilliance, thunderbolts; moonlight, sunrise, sunset, lustrelessness, darkness." And this could describe *Prometheus*, where Scriabin spoke of its rays of light, lightning flashes, and glowing cosmic mists and clarifications.

Prometheus: the Poem of Fire is the most densely Theosophical piece of music ever written. Its symbolism is endless. The opening six-note chord represents Original Chaos, the universe before lives have been lived and destiny or rebirths accumulated. The first theme intones the Creative Principle. The instant of fire-giving is suddenly announced by a succession of four chords of open fourths in the trumpets, followed instantly by the solo trumpet theme of Will, a gradual ascension of increasingly wider intervals. Then begins the equanimous theme, Dawn of Human Consciousness, which Scriabin sometimes called "Reason."

The piano represents Man or the microcosm, and it appears imperiously playing the trumpet's earlier Will theme. The orchestra symbolizes the Cosmos or the macrocosm. At [2] in the score, the Joy of Life theme (Scriabin also called it the "Dance of Self-Discovery") appears in the piano, one of Scriabin's fragmentary waltz rhythms, formed from the tag end of the Dawn of Human Consciousness theme. At [3] the piano, in another waltz rhythm, describes the theme of Play of the Creative Spirit or theme of Activity and Movement. The descent of a minor ninth interval, which Scriabin marks with stresses, points out the moment that spirit descends into matter. At [9] the piano grandly takes over the Creative Principle theme which then becomes Ego. Matter has now become spirit, hence its modulation a perfect fourth higher in pitch.

All the melodies and themes derive from the initial harmony—there are eleven mottoes or motifs in all—and they signify variously sexual languor, magical exorcism, the stopping of time, etc. The violin and flute alternately represent human emotion or feeling rhapsodically afire.

Throughout the entire composition Scriabin concerned himself with the descent of spirit into matter, or "materialization," and the transformation of matter into original spirit, light, flashes, or "dematerialization." Constantly there is countervailing movement, Brahmanical breathing in and breathing out, impression and expression, involution and evolution. In the end, incarnated Spirit or Soul is re-released into the ether as pure disembodiment, nirvana or cosmic dust, wind- and star-swept, blown by solar winds and galactic orgasms of ecstasy.

The chorus enters with its non-meaning sounds—humming and ah,e,o,ho—signifying the inarticulate cry of the newborn baby, the outbreak from unity into multiplicity, the step from man to Mankind. The work's final phrase of rising, open fourths, first adumbrated in *Ecstasy*, now is developed as an independent theme of Self-affirmation, or "I am."

Scriabin referred to "Prometheus" equally as Satan and Lucifer, suggesting the demonic side of his nature and his music. These three figures of religion and history were all "light bringers" like Scriabin. When Satan fell from the sky he made a streak of lightning. Archangel Lucifer was the Morning Star in the heavens. Prometheus, of course, stole sparks of the gods' chariot wheels as they rumbled through the firmament and gave the fire to man down on earth below. Scriabin loved these three archrebels who, by defying God, enabled man to equal, then surpass God Himself. With this supremacy, Scriabin found himself altogether congenial.

XI In Performance

Scriabin made a tremendous reputation for himself as a concert performer. This fact is all the more surprising when one remembers that his time was the golden era of Russian pianism. Pianistic geniuses flourished, as they do now again in Soviet Russia. Although Scriabin never played any music but his own after his graduation recital, he was still a pianist in the accepted sense. Only from the spring of 1902 until April of 1905—for three years—was Scriabin ever absent from the recital hall.

Moreover, Scriabin from very early years was in competition with the greatest pianists of the day who also played his music. Josef Lhevinne began playing Scriabin in 1896, and introduced a set of études to his Paris audiences. The great pianist Konstantin Igumnov also played Scriabin from that same year on, and there were others among the stars promoting Scriabin—Josef Hofmann, Ivanovskaya-Zalesskaya, Felix Blumenfeld (as pianist, not conductor), and de Conne. Fyodor Keneman even played the First Sonata for his graduation recital in 1895.

Later, supreme virtuosi of the caliber of Vsevolod Buyu-

kli, Mark Meichik, Elena Bekman-Shcherbina and Samuel
Feinberg, studied specific compositions with Scriabin and
introduced them to the public in Russia and abroad. Bekman-Shcherbina, for example, despite her small hands gave
the first performance of the Sixth Sonata, a composition
which contains some of the widest, most hand-spanning
sounds ever written without arpeggiation. Scriabin himself
did not like anyone's performance of his piano music, and
said so privately. His friends, however, pleased him in their
interpretation of certain pieces, "but certain pieces only,"
as Delson emphasizes. Inconsistently, Scriabin enjoyed any
orchestral performance of his music, no matter how medio-
cre the orchestra and conductor might have been.

There can be no question that Scriabin as a performer
suffered from certain defects. It is interesting to compare
two comments about Scriabin. Both say, in essence, the
same thing. First, here is Belaieff in a confidential letter
to Safonov reporting on how their protégé was received in
St. Petersburg, where at the age of twenty-three in 1895 he
had just made his début.

Belaieff is writing, naturally, about a very young man—
and people were younger in those days than they are now.

> As a performer he is regarded less trustfully than as a com-
> poser. It seems to me that this is not without foundation. Is
> this the result of his nervousness? Is it because he never plays
> with partners but always solo? Sometimes he confuses the
> auditor by the way he ruffles through a piece. You can't fol-
> low either the melody or the meter, and there seems, some-
> times, to be a kind of studied affectation about the way he
> plays. This is not his true nature. My desire is for him to play
> his music so superbly that his performances will create a
> tradition for posterity.

Now, contrast this with a review of Scriabin's last appearance in Moscow in 1915. The distinguished Grigori

Prokofiev, critic for the *Russian Musical Gazette,* by no
means entirely partial to Scriabin, though beamish, reported
as follows:

> . . . great success and the impression that lingers is one of
> ravishment. What makes Scriabin's music "ravishing" is
> simply the enchantment of his performance. The tone is
> marvelous, despite a continuous sharpness, even clanging
> *mezzo piano,* but he achieves extraordinary effects. Don't
> forget he is a wizard with the pedal, though his ethereal
> sounds cannot quite fill the hall. He captivates his audience,
> too, by giving the impression of improvising. He breaks the
> rhythmic flow and something new comes out each time. This
> suffuses the performance with freshness. Never has he played
> his Fourth Sonata with more mastery or sincerity as he did
> yesterday. What power he put in the theme in the second
> movement! Yet the *actual* sound was not big. The secret is in
> the energetic rhythm.

We see here how the playing, the performance by Scriabin, is the same at the end of his life, as it was in the beginning. But finally, all his failings of impulsiveness have been
transcended somehow, transmuted into plus points instead
of minus marks. Still, Scriabin's own way of playing is
a dangerous path for a performing artist to enter.

Tatyana Shaborkina, Director of the Scriabin Museum,
in 1940 wrote an interesting article on "Scriabin the Performer." Her method was to tabulate all the reviews ever
written of Scriabin concerts and to extrapolate the descriptions most often made regarding his playing. These were
"arhythmical," "nervous," "magical," "wizard-like colors,"
"pedalization," "tonal lights," "pauses," and "silences full
of thought." In trying to copy these notable aspects of the
composer's own playing, the performer risks mannerism for
manner, idiosyncrasy for personality, affectation for affect,
and artifice for art, let it be warned.

In Scriabin's own lifetime, many mistook the mirage of his performance for an oasis. It comes as a shock to today's listener to hear "Scriabin Plays," transcriptions of his own performances from his Welte-Mignon piano rolls issued by the Ministry of Culture. (Melodiya D 00031359-60.) The playing is extraordinarily erratic, arhythmical, nervous, and, of course, because it is reconstructed music, the pedalization belongs to the engineers rather than to Scriabin himself.

In any event, Scriabin called the art of performance "the art of experience." He said that "a composition is many facetted . . . alive and breathes on its own. It is one thing today, and another tomorrow, like the sea. How awful it would be if the sea were the same every day and the same forever, like a movie film!" Yavorsky bears out this concept of shifting performances. Since he was a serious student of Scriabin in concert and attended each performance with the music in his hands, a critic in 1913 asked him about the variations in Scriabin's own performances. "Scriabin always plays more or less as he has written his pieces. On occasions he plays them entirely different . . . and opposite from the way they are marked," Yavorsky answered, and added, "More important is that when he changes them, it is always for the best." When Scriabin's alterations in the scores were pointed out to him, one time, he was surprised and then laughed, saying, "Well, changes are permitted the composer."

Scriabin has had much written about him as a performer. Sabaneeff best expressed the unusual quality of his playing by calling it "a secret liturgical act." He said that even "passive, unconditioned listeners" felt "electric currents touching their psyche," as Scriabin performed his music. "This was not simply an artistic experience, but something quite irrational, something that really crossed over the frontiers of art as we think of it. . . ." His playing, apparently, was "ineffable" or *inafferando*, as he marked his famous theme-song, the Poem Op. 32 No. 1. As such, it was inexplicable in its effect.

In 1916 in Petrograd, a leading piano teacher, N. N. Cherkass, published a monograph, *Scriabin as Pianist and Piano Composer*. It is the sort of book a biographer dreams of, for here is a man whose credentials were impeccable (he was a pioneer in scientific pianism, muscular relaxation, playing from the back and shoulders instead of merely with the fingers), and who wrote honestly without prejudice or predilection. In those times in Russia it was almost impossible to see the tree of Scriabin the pianist for the forest of his ideas and the glamor of his personality.

Immediately, Cherkass wrote, "The world has lost one of its greatest masters of music!" and then goes on to comment on the "unprecedented, unbridled worship of Scriabin after his death . . . except for the critics belonging to the extreme right wing." He also describes the spell Scriabin cast during the last years of his life. At one concert Scriabin played badly, so badly, that the person sitting next to Cherkass said to his friend, "Some places are so wild I think the composer is mocking the public." The companion answered, "How can anyone this famous play badly!"

Cherkass continues, "The memory of Scriabin as a composer will remain unchanged for centuries, thanks to the worth of his music. But the truth about Scriabin the pianist has already begun to fade, and the historian of the future will come to conclusions that are wrong . . . I know that many people will not be pleased by my releasing this monograph to the world. I have approached my subject from a new viewpoint, and I hope that my vision will become the property of the future."

Cherkass attributes the beginning of the Scriabin mys-

tique not only to postmortem deification but to his success
in America. "We know how backward Americans are musically . . . barely out of the Beethoven stage," and he finds
it extraordinary that they took to Scriabin. (Actually, Scriabin's "success" was more in Russian journals than in American ones, as it had been in England in 1914.)

The core of Cherkass's book is in italics: *"Scriabin was
a bad pianist."* The author continued to explain why. He
described Scriabin's awkward walk to the piano as he
came out on stage. Clearly he was "a sick man, with an
inner sickness that disturbed his entire nervous system"
and made his "musculature abnormal." As he played, he
tensed his entire body (which is why he was so physically
exhausted after concerts) and made muscular compensa-
tions which distorted not only his appearance but his sounds.
His fingers moved, in short, incorrectly. This "muffled and
dampened" his tone, and the improper tension and muscular contraction of his hands and arms prevented a proper
legato connection of tones, and impeded a correct staccato.
These "defects of technique" affected the nuances of his
playing and limited the degree to which he could increase
or diminish his tonal level. . . . *piano* and *forte.*

Cherkass gives an example from the Ninth Sonata where
Scriabin has marked *pp crescendo poco a poco.* Scriabin
played the episode *forte* and the only increase in sound
came from the left hand.

37

One method of compensating for these muscular defects was Scriabin's excessive *rubato*. But Cherkass placed Scriabin as a child of his century of pianists, and attributes the "affectation" of so much *rubato* to "Jewish pianists and Jewish teachers." "Scriabin received his musical training in the atmosphere of deformed rhythm, absorbed it despite his musical sensitivity, and allowed it to spoil his rhythmic taste." Even within one measure Scriabin could not play metrically. His rhythms zigzagged. As an example he cites the Etude Op. 8 No. 12. It is written:

38a

Scriabin, however, actually played it in performance this way, giving it, as Cherkass says, "a most inconclusive, dilettante effect":

38b

Cherkass dryly warns that Scriabin's own "performances should not be the authority for playing his music . . . better pianists can better sculpture his music." As for Scriabin's pedalization, Cherkass is blunt. "He took his foot off the pedal only to put it down again, but in rare instances played entirely without pedal." This was because of his faulty *legato*. Had he been capable of a correct *legato*, he would not have overused the pedal, he says.

When it came to displaying harmony at the piano, Scriabin, Cherkass says, "had an amazing ability. His innate sensitivity to harmonic clarity kept him in line . . . He could separate voices clearly." He quotes a critic who once said, "When you look at Scriabin's harmonies, they seem muddled and yet, when you hear him play, they for some reason sound clear."

Cherkass pinpoints the "most important question for the artistic interpretation of Scriabin's music." He centers it, rather circumlocutiously, in "the dynamic relative shading [balance of tones] within a simultaneous concord of voices," meaning the inner tonal emphasis of any given, single harmony contained in a passage of Scriabin music. Here, of course, the composer excelled, because he knew what sound effect he wanted. Cherkass also notes that Scriabin had "a colossal muscular memory . . . played accurately and without note mistakes," which, of course, defines one kind of virtuosity.

Cherkass, doubtless, gives us an academic portrait of Scriabin in performance. Only the "magic" of his playing is missing. Whether Scriabin was pedagogically legitimate as a pianist or not, he managed to create the impression on his listeners of combining the sheen of pearls with the sparkle of diamonds. Many of Scriabin's contemporaries refused to hear any pianist but the composer himself play his own music.

Prokofiev in his autobiography contrasts Rachmaninov and Scriabin as performers. "When Scriabin played the Fifth Sonata every note soared. With Rachmaninov all the notes lay on the ground." He describes an incident in 1915 in St. Petersburg on the occasion of Rachmaninov's final all-Scriabin recital. His performance caused considerable agitation among those who adored—and had known— the composer. Ivan Alchevsky, leading tenor at the Maryinsky Opera, and an idolator of Scriabin, at the end of Rachmaninov's program said aloud, "I'm going backstage to tell him how the Fifth *should* be played." Proko-

fiev tried to be objective and pointed out that, "Although
we are used to Scriabin's own playing and, naturally, preferred it, obviously there are other possible interpretations
and styles." He held Alchevsky by the jacket trying to re-
strain him, but was dragged along to the artist's room.
Alchevsky grabbed Rachmaninov and shouted at him.

"After this dreadful explosion I tried to soothe the ruffled
Rachmaninov. 'All the same, Sergei Vassilievich,' I said,
'you played it very well.' Rachmaninov froze in his tracks.
'You, you Sergei Sergeievich, thought I could actually play
badly?!' " Prokofiev and Rachmaninov were never again
friendly.

This question of interpretation and the whole arena of
liberties an interpretive artist can take with a composer's
music is vexing. For example, Julius Isserlis was once presented to Scriabin as a young aspiring pianist. He played
one of the Op. 11 Preludes. Scriabin spoke out midway
through, "You're playing it at half tempo." Isserlis stopped
playing and looked at the composer. "This is *my* interpretation of the music." Scriabin snapped back, "But it's *my*
music," his eyes roving planets away.

A similar distortion of Scriabin music also belongs to
Rachmaninov. The only piece of Scriabin's Rachmaninov
ever recorded (although he taught the Eighth Sonata to
Gina Bachauer and occasionally played the Fantasy Op. 28
in concert) was the Prelude Op. 11 No. 8 in F♯ Minor. It
is marked *Allegro Agitato* and the metronome marking
Scriabin gave the piece (at Belaieff's insistence) clearly in-
dicates the speed and drama he wished from it. However,
Rachmaninov played the piece as if it were a very slow
Lento, which turned into something wistful, a wisp of
nostalgia.*

* This recording is available from the International Piano Library, 215
West 91st Street, New York City 10024.

Looking at Scriabin compositions, we see at every turn
how he worked for non-piano effects, to make the piano a
kind of celestial orchestra of unearthly sounds. His first
task was, invariably, how to defy the piano's laws—how to
keep its evanescent tone from dissipating into the air, how
to give the impression that piano strings can hold a note at
the same intensity with which it starts, how to make the
resonance last, and last, and last. The pedal sustains only
the initial impact, the first of a series of rapidly diminishing
decibels of sounds. Scriabin constantly devised extended fig-
urations to prevent this—trills, reiterated arpeggi, repeated
chords, and melodic lines intensified by clusters of notes
which flicker like fires to radiate steady heat.

In brief, Scriabin wanted the sound of the breeze through
a pine tree as it would appear in a painting, or the look of
a poem on music paper in sound. He considered music to
be like prisms of crystals reflecting and refracting thousands
of lights and colors. He strove to remove the human coeffi-
cient from music, so that all that was left would be purest,
blinding, most radiant light . . . the light which man himself is when the "angel within unsheathes."

And these, indeed, are impossible demands to make on
pianists, demands which Scriabin, as if by sleight of hand,
appeared to have achieved during his lifetime, according to
some. They supply today's artists perpetual difficulties . . .
because they are, after all, ideals, and ideals are not necessarily reality, past or future.

Bibliography

A. Alshvang. *Izbrannyye Sochinyeniya.* Muzyka. Moscow. 1964.
F. Bowers. *Scriabin.* Kodansha International Ltd. Tokyo and Palo Alto. 1969.
E. Carpenter. *Thematic Development and Continuity in the Ten Piano Sonatas of Alexander Scriabin.* Kent State University. 1972.
N. Cherkass. *Skryabin Kak Pianist i Fortepiannyi Kompozitor.* Petrograd. 1916.
L. Danilevich. *A. N. Skryabin.* Muzgiz. Moscow. 1953.
V. Delson. *Skryabin.* Muzyka. Moscow. 1971.
V. Dernova. *Garmoniya Skryabina.* Muzyka. Leningrad. 1968.
A. Kashperov. *Skryabin. Pis'ma.* Muzyka. Moscow. 1965.
E. Kaufman. *The Evolution of Form and Technique in the Late Works of Scriabin.* Yale University. 1972.
M. Mikhailov. *A. N. Skryabin.* Muzyka. Moscow/Leningrad. 1966.
Muzyka i Sovryemyennost'. Muzyka. Moscow. 1969.
S. Pavchinsky. *Proizvyedyeniya Skryabina Pozdnyevo Perioda.* Muzyka. Moscow. 1969.
S. Randlett. *The Nature and Development of Scriabin's Pianistic Vocabulary.* Northwestern University. 1966.
L. Sabaneeff. *Vospominaniye o Skryabinye.* Muzsektor. Moscow. 1925.
Skryabin. Gosudarstvyennoye Izdatyel'stvo. Petrograd. 1923.
O. Saklaltuycva. *O Garmoniya Skryabina.* Muzyka. Moscow. 1965.
Sbornik. State Music Publishers. Moscow/Leningrad. 1940.
B. Schloezer. *A. Skryabin.* Grani. Berlin. 1923.
H. Steger. *Der Weg der Klaviersonaten bei Alexander Skryabin.* Wollen-weber. Munich. 1972.
B. Yavorsky. Volume I. *Vospominaniya, Stat i, Perepiska.* Volume II. *Izbrannyye Trudy.* (Edited by D. Shostakovich) Soyuzkniga. 1971/2.
D. Zhitomirskii. *Russkiye Kompozitory.* Sovyetskii Kompozitor. Moscow. 1960.

Index

207